Mordecai Richler, bestselling author of *Cocksure* and other novels, turns his ironic eye to the facts of life around him – from Expo 67 through Norman Mailer, Jews in Sport, Tarzan of the Apes, and numerous other stopovers – and finds them as strange as anything in fiction. So he coldly and mordantly shoots them down.

The result is, in *Hunting Tigers Under Glass*, 'a marvellously clear-sighted attack' (*The Guardian*) 'by an acute, highly modern mind' (*Evening Standard*) displaying 'formidable turns of anger wherever national or racial pretensions are a blind merely for stupidity and intolerance' (*The Spectator*).

Although Richler is consistently unsentimental – or perhaps *because* he is consistently unsentimental – belly laughs come thick and fast.

Also by Mordecai Richler in Panther Books

Cocksure
Son of a Smaller Hero

Mordecai Richler

Hunting Tigers
Under Glass

essays and reports

Panther

Granada Publishing Limited
Published in 1971 by Panther Books Ltd
3 Upper James Street, London W1R 4BP

First published by Weidenfeld & Nicolson Ltd 1969
Copyright © Mordecai Richler 1968
Made and printed in Great Britain by
C. Nicholls & Company Ltd
The Philips Park Press, Manchester
Set in Monotype Garamond

Contents

Acknowledgements

These essays and reports first appeared, sometimes in a slightly different form, in the *New York Review of Books*, *Commentary*, *Encounter*, *Book Week*, the *New Statesman*, the *London Magazine*, *Holiday*, and *Macleans*. I would like to thank the editors for permission to reprint them here.

Edmund Wilson's Canada, Paper Lion, and Expo Exposed, reprinted from the *New York Review of Books*, Copyright © 1965, 1967, *The New York Review*. Koufax The Incomparable, reprinted from *Commentary*, Copyright © 1966, Mordecai Richler. This Year In Jerusalem, With The Trail Smoke Eaters in Stockholm, reprinted from *Macleans*, 1961, 1962, Copyright © Mordecai Richler. Hold That Lineage! reprinted from *Book Week*, Copyright © 1966. Jewish Writing reprinted from the *New Statesman*, Copyright © 1967. The Catskills: Land of Milk and Money, reprinted from *Holiday*, Copyright © 1965. Mailer reprinted from *Encounter*, Copyright © 1965. Letter From Canada reprinted from *London Magazine*, Copyright © 1968.   M.R.

for Bob and Audrey Weaver
and my other friends
in Toronto –
the Lefoliis and Fulfords,
Kildare and Mary,
J.G. MCCL., and Sir Casimir's
grandson Pete

These essays and reports, written over seven years, are knit with three themes: Jewish experience, a concern with literary matters, and the changing Canadian scene. More often than not, the themes are entwined, which is only natural. After all, I'm a Jewish writer from Canada.

The fact that I am a Canadian Jewish writer may seem so obvious as to be unworthy of comment, but, fifteen years ago, when I first began to publish, it troubled me enormously.

Because I didn't want to be taken for that pathetic provincial, the Canadian writer, I wouldn't allow my first novel to be compromised by the imprint of a Toronto publisher and went out of my way to have *The Acrobats* published in England.

Neither, I now recall with embarrassment, did I wish to be classified as a Jewish writer. No, no. I was, as I pompously protested to an interviewer, a writer who merely happened to be Jewish.

Fortunately for me, a Yiddish newspaper in Montreal saw the interview and swiftly cut me down to size: 'The oven is big, the loaf is small.'

To be a Jew and a Canadian is to emerge from the ghetto twice, for self-conscious Canadians, like some touchy Jews, tend to contemplate the world through a wrong-ended telescope, as witness what is still my most cherished Canadian newspaper headline: 1960 WAS A GOOD YEAR FOR PLAYWRIGHTS FROM OUTSIDE OF CANADA. Like Jews again, Canadians are inclined to regard with a mixture of envy and suspicion those who have forsaken the homestead (or *shtetl*) for the assimilationist flesh-pots of New York or London. And so, on visits home, I am vulnerable to two-pronged (and contradictory) attacks.

Once, after speaking at a suburban synagogue, I was asked, 'Why is it that everybody loved Sholem Aleichem, but we all hate you? Because you're a stinker who writes garbage about your people.'

Later the same night, at a WASP party, somebody asked me, 'When are you going to stop writing sentimental stuff about the Jews and write something about Canadians?' Real Canadians.

Enraged letters come from both camps. After a piece on Jewish matters, '. . . I really must say that I feel you couldn't have done a better job of anti-semitic propaganda if you had been Oswald Mosley himself. Perhaps you are? It would be a brilliant stroke for any Fascist to take a Jewish name as a *nom de plume* . . .' But following an essay that ridiculed a number of Canadian pretensions, '. . . probably you aren't a Canadian anyway with THAT name!'

A piece I wrote, included in this collection, about *The Encyclopedia of Jews in Sport,* brought more than one reader to the boil. The piece, unmistakably comic in intention, ended,

> 'I, for one, look forward to an encyclopedia (for delinquent Bar Mitzvah boys perhaps) on Jewish Drunks, High School Dropouts and Junkies From Noah to Today. I would also like to see a compilation of Famous Jewish Homosexuals, Professional and Amateur, Through History.'

'With what end in view Mr. Richler?' a reader wrote. 'To stir the embers into flame of latent anti-semitism anew? To give the psychopaths and rabid racists yet another stick to beat the Jews with? If you are serious you could have no thought or feeling for your fellow man. If you meant it as a joke, it's damned unfunny. In any case you are too late, forty years late, and twenty years late for Maidaneck, Belsen and Auschwitz . . .'

Another essay, included in this volume, which poked fun at the more outlandish Canadian centennial projects, also provoked an inflamed letter. 'Canada's Centennial Year – and maybe Expo '67 – seems to be bringing out the worst in (some) Canadians. The only people putting the skids under Canada are some Canadians themselves – why, why, why? . . . I'm glad you feel you've paid a considerable price for leaving Canada. My husband also left Canada – in December, 1939, to fight as a Canadian – along with thousands of others – PROUD to be a Canadian, and boy how some people thought them big-headed then for being proud of Canada and being Canadian AND shouting about it – good for them – and like thousands of them, he was not able to return – he was killed in action. NOW, all these men of BOTH World Wars are being "stabbed in the back" by their own countrymen – their lives have obviously been given in vain . . .'

Occasionally wires cross. A Jewish reader will protest against my attitude to things Canadian. 'Don't they hate us enough, the bastards, without you making fun, stirring them up . . .' Or a liberal Gentile reader will deplore my outlook on Jewish matters. 'It makes it so much harder for we poor deluded Jewish apologists to defend the Jews against the various charges traditionally laid against them by anti-semites . . .'

At a conference called in Toronto, in 1961, to measure the progress of the arts in Canada, a distinguished Canadian educator denounced from the platform those expatriate Canadians who wrote denigrating articles about Canada for *recherché* British magazines. (The *Spectator*, actually.) Just as some of the boys I grew up with have privately allowed that I'm not an anti-Semite out of conviction, but for profit's sake, imagining that I am beseiged in toilets by vicious goy editors who offer me bundles of money if only I will write some thing inflammatory about the Jews, so this educator went on to say how it was well-known that British periodicals lusted for articles knocking Canada and were prepared to fork out vast sums to turncoats.

Say, £25 from the *Spectator* or *New Statesman*, and maybe £50 from *Encounter*.

If these essays and reports reflect three themes, sometimes commingled, then it is also true to say that they are bound by a unifying tone of voice. A certain scepticism, a tendency to deflate. And so perhaps those readers who never write shrill letters will pardon me if I make a flat statement for the benefit of those who do. I am not an anti-Canadian or a Jew-baiter. I do, however, deplore many things Jewish and Canadian. Special pleading, whether by Canadian sports writers in Stockholm, kibbutzniks in Galilee, or proliferating Canada culture boosters, never fails to move me to mockery.

All the same, it's possible that my timing is bad. *Or is it?*

'This Year in Jerusalem', for instance, is a journal based on a month's travel in Israel in 1962. At the time it seemed permissible to laugh, if only not to weep, at the attitude of a kibbutznik – in this case, a Canadian who had quit Canada because of anti-Semitism – towards the Arabs.

'The trouble with the Arabs', he said, 'is they won't mix. They're private. They stick to their own people and areas. Another thing, you know, is they have loyalties outside the country.'

If I enjoyed myself in Zion, I was not entirely at ease. I was upset by a not uncommon Israeli arrogance. Take the bartender at the Hotel Eilat, for example. He told me, 'One day I served a Spaniard here. A rich man. He said that in Madrid he was an anti-Semite. He said, I didn't believe these Jews could ever build a country so I thought I'd see for myself. Well, now I've seen the country, he said, and it's marvellous. It wouldn't surprise me if you people had the atom bomb in five years and took over the Middle East in ten. But you're not Jews; you're different. You've fought for your land, you've spilled blood for it, and you have pride. The Jews in

Spain would only fight for their families and their businesses. You're different here, he said,' the bartender repeated with approval.

At the time, I was infuriated. After all, a number of Jews in Spain would not only fight for their families and businesses, but also happened to have fought for the Republic, as did Jews from other countries with the International Brigade.

Since my stay in Israel, however, there has been the Six Day War; and the Israelis, some contemptuous of the Arabs, others arrogant, have won a famous victory. A victory I, a Diaspora Jew, cheered from a safe distance.

Given today's nervy conditions in the Middle East, neither peace nor war, some, I'm sure, would consider it in exceedingly bad taste to publish criticisms of Israel. I, on the other hand, consider it more pertinent than ever before.

The explicitly Canadian pieces in this collection, 'O Canada' and 'Expo', could provoke the same order of response. In Canada, at least.

I wrote 'Expo' after a visit to Montreal in June 1967, a week before de Gaulle came to town, a time when Separatism, after the bombs of 1963, seemed to have dwindled. Mistakenly, I then took it to be no more than a fringe issue. In the piece, written for *The New York Review of Books*, I repeated a joke a friend had told me to illustrate what had become of English-speaking Canada's haste to hire French Canadians, sometimes indiscriminately.

A man sitting by a pool sees a lady drowning. 'Help, help,' she cries. The man rushes over to the French Canadian lifeguard and shouts, 'Aren't you going to do anything?' 'I can't swim,' he says. 'What! You're a lifeguard and you can't swim?' 'I don't have to. I'm bilingual.'

Since then, René Levesque, one of the country's most admirable politicians, has left the Liberal party and declared himself a Separatist; and General de Gaulle has spoken once more, this time from Paris. On my last visit to Ottawa, in

December 1967, I was astonished to discover that the most thoughtful people now took Separatism to be a distinct possibility.

If that's the case, I consider this the best possible time to protest English-speaking Canada's fatuity, and its continuing inadequate response to French Canada's aspirations. If only because I, for one, would be immensely saddened if Canada were to fragment and become a North American Balkans.

Finally, as I am a writer vain enough to think my real office is to write fiction, these essays represent time out, as does my work in films. With this essential difference. I usually write films for profit, but these essays were all written for my own pleasure. And education. If I'm able to communicate just some of my enjoyment of Israel, the Catskills, comic books, Jews in sport, and the Canadian comedy, to readers, then I will count this collection a success.

LONDON

JANUARY 1968

Last year (L.B.J. willing, French Canada permitting) Canada was a hundred years old and this, *The Unknown Country, The Golden Hinge, The Uneasy Neighbour, The Giant of the North*, was transmogrified, albeit along decent Presbyterian lines, into a Disneyland that rocked'n'rolled from coast to coast. Put plainly, there was not a township so small or a city so cynical that it could risk being caught without a centennial project. Some of the schemes, like Montreal's Expo' 67, were grand, indeed, even if the freshness of conception ('The theme of Expo' 67 will be: "MAN AND HIS WORLD" ') didn't exactly hit you bang in the eye. Other municipal projects, among the 2000 approved, included a centennial salmon-spawning channel. And just in case the sapients on your town council failed to come up with something sufficiently fetching, then, waiting to guide you in Toronto, rather like glorified barmitzvah caterers, there was a centennial advisory company. Among hotsy projects undertaken, one, by the Federated Women's Institutes of Canada, sponsored a competition for a centennial poem and another, this from our very own Imperial Order of the Daughters of the Empire (I.O.D.E.), announced a contest for the best novel or play 'set in one of Canada's provinces as it is today or was in the past.' *Canadian Municipal Utilities*, a trade journal, suggested 'it would be a very fitting Birthday Present for a municipality to have a water system or sewage treatment plant in 1967 . . . Canada's people in 1967 may not think of the Fathers of Confederation each time they wash their hands or flush a toilet, but. . . .'

Meanwhile Canada remains a loosely-knit, all but unmanageable confederation. There is trouble, trouble everywhere. 'There is no Canadian nation,' Marcel Chaput, a

French-Canadian Separatist leader, has written. 'There is a Canadian state (which is) a purely political and artificial entity. . . .' French Canada, quiescent for years, is in a turmoil. John Diefenbaker's inept, but comic, federal government has been displaced by an equally inept and scandal-ridden government, this one led by Lester Pearson, of whom so much was hoped. Industry and natural resources everywhere are too often American-owned. And sadly it is not only our iron and copper ore that is going down to the States, but also, at the alarming rate of 50,000 a year, some of the people most crucial to Canada's development. Scientists, engineers, doctors, and businessmen, too many of whom are understandably drawn to what Morley Callaghan has called 'the sources of light'.

This is the climate then in which Canadians have become increasingly anxious to discover within themselves a culture-cum-national identity that amounts to something less nebulous than being nicer than Americans and not as snobby as the British; and the protracted search has made for many changes since I first left Canada in 1954.

At the time, it seemed to many observers, myself included, that the country was starved for culture, and nothing could be worse. How foolish we were. For now that the country is culture-crazed and more preoccupied than ever before with its own absence of a navel, how one yearns for Canada's engaging buckeye suspicion of art and artists of not so long ago. I was brought up in a folksy Canada. I remember the bad old days when it was necessary to come to the defence of artistic youngsters, and we suffered a wave of enlightened CBC radio and TV plays which educated the public to the fact that we were not all notoriously heavy drinkers, like William Faulkner, or queers, like Jean Genet. We strung words together sort of, but we were regular fellers: Canadians. In a typical play a sensitive little twerp named David or Christopher, usually son of a boorish insurance agent, roused his dad's ire because he wouldn't play hockey or hit back. Instead he was studying piano with an effeminate Frenchman or painting with a tricksy Hungarian Jew ('A piece of blank paper! Mit a brush und paints, vot an opportunity for beauty!') and in the end made dad eat his words by winning the piano competition in Toronto or, if the writer was inclined to irony, by being commissioned to paint a mural for the new skyscraper being built by the insurance company dad worked for.

– That's some kid you've got there, Henry. When it comes to splashing paint on walls he's a real home-run hitter.

– Gosh.

When I was a student there was actually a course on Can. lit. at Sir George Williams U., but the text was mimeographed and a typical assignment was for a student to list all the books ever written about the Hudson's Bay Co., noting the dimensions, number of pages, and photographs. Now there are a number of books, most of them embarrassingly boosterish, about Canadian writing, and there is at least one serious quarterly, the bi-lingual *Canadian Literature*, edited by George Woodcock, that is exclusively – no, quixotically – devoted to the study of Canadian writing past and present. In the very first issue Dwight Macdonald, asked to appraise a number of Canadian little magazines, was left with the impression of 'a starved, pinched version of our own culture'. Canada, he felt, was 'a mingy version of the United States'. That was 1959. Since then a real Canadian book club has been formed, with monthly selections that run from Malcolm Lowry's *Ultramarine* to *Love and Peanut Butter* ('Lesley Conger's warm and lively account of the trials of being a wife, mother and writer in a wild Vancouver household.'); and there is a worthy and useful paperback library of Canadian, um, classics. Blue chip Leacocks, some good Callaghans, and rather too many of our frontier day unreadables indecently exhumed. In fact today the cultural heat is such that the shrewd downtown grocer who has survived supermarket competition must now live through another crisis: the spade-bearded entrepreneur who wants to buy out the lease and convert the premises into an art gallery. Instead of Libby's soup and Kellogg's Super 'K', pictures of Libby's soup and Kellogg's Super 'K'. If when I was a student there was something shamefully un-Presbyterian in admitting you were a writer, today to merely let on that you're 'creative' is to stand back and duck a shower of prizes and offers, and to enjoy a nice little side income in supplying radio and TV stations with your outspoken opinions on divorce, household pets, masturbation, and the Bomb (a shadow we live under).

There are rather more art than harvest festivals in Canada these days and variations on a seminar I attended in Toronto in 1961 ('to measure Canada's national cultural development in relation to other nations') are plentiful. A recent edition of the Entertainments supplement to the Saturday edition of the Montreal *Star* lists no less than fifty art galleries in its calendar of events. The calendar also informs readers that this is 'Liberal Judaism Week' and *afficionados* can hear Rabbi H. Leonard Poller discuss 'Count Up, Count Down, What Does the Liberal Jew Count?' An ad in the same edition runs,

SOMETHING MISSING?

What do Vancouver, Winnipeg, Toronto, Ottawa (soon) and Halifax have that Montreal hasn't. A professional English language theatre, that's what! Want to do something to help change this terrible situation? Send your name to...

All of which goes to prove that Canadian culture, and criticism thereof, is clearly a growth industry, though it always seemed to me to be one of the few that was proof against an American takeover bid. Then, in 1960, Edmund Wilson wrote in the *New Yorker* that Morley Callaghan 'is today perhaps the most unjustly neglected novelist in the English-speaking world' and that here was a writer 'whose work may be mentioned without absurdity in association with Chekhov's and Turgenev's'. A shot that ricochetted through all the universities on the northerly side of the world's largest unarmed frontier and sent critics scrambling after the Callaghan novels . . . only to report back that they still found them wanting.

Then it was rumoured that Mr. Wilson was in Montreal, he had actually been seen in Toronto, and was working on a book about Canadian writing. (Canadian writing, for Christ's sake! Edmund Wilson!) Now *O Canada! An American's Notes on Canadian Culture* has at last been published. *O CANADA, O EDMUND WILSON, O NUTS*, ran a review headline in the Toronto *Telegram*, which now reports on books as well as axe-murders, and underneath somebody called Michael Bawtree wrote, 'not quite my idea of criticism.' H.L.M. of the Windsor *Star* agreed. Taking issue with Mr. Wilson's evaluation of Callaghan, he wrote, 'Much more can be learned about Canada from the writings of Thomas Costain, who isn't mentioned.' H.L.M. also did not concur with Mr. Wilson's opinion that Canadian criticism tended to be provincial. 'In the main it probably doesn't go along with the presumption that if a book is dirty enough, it's good enough, in fact superior.'

Well, well. But this is really no more bumpkinish than reviews in too many American newspapers and the truth is not all Canadian criticism comes off the cob. Some of our most discerning critics (George Woodcock, Robert Fulford) found much to admire in Mr. Wilson's book, but they were also troubled by other aspects of it. Speaking for myself, I'm more than an admirer of Mr. Wilson, I've been a grateful addict for years, but I felt let down by *O Canada*. Maybe the trouble was I approached the book too much in the spirit of the hero of Walker Percy's *The Movie-Goer*, who could not feel his district was real until it was put on the silver screen. Unfortunately, not even Mr. Wilson could make Can. lit. real for me. *O Canada*, especially in its discussion of the French, is acute, even illuminating at times, but elsewhere it is too often cursory, and Edmund Wilson's approach to Canadian culture suffers from being filtered through a romantic American lens, a nostalgia for things past. I will return to this point later. Meanwhile, some notes on Mr. Wilson's notes.

MORLEY CALLAGHAN. It is Mr. Wilson's opinion that Callaghan has been unjustly neglected by his compatriots, possibly because it is difficult for them to imagine a writer of such stature living amongst them, and also because 'literary mediocrity is predisposed to be spiteful to talent.' Yes, yes, but it is not Canadians who have for so long neglected Callaghan, surely our most talented writer, but rather the Americans and the British. Years ago Malcolm Cowley wondered (in *Exile's Return*, I think) whatever became of Morley Callaghan, and Mr. Wilson himself observes that after Callaghan returned to Canada in the late thirties he was 'quickly forgotten in the United States . . . and almost unknown in England.' In all that time, Canadian publishers continued to keep Callaghan's novels and collected stories in print and serious Canadian critics continued to regard him very highly indeed. During Mr. Callaghan's lean period the CBC helped to sustain him with non-literary work (panel shows, interview programmes) and *Maclean's* awarded him a $5,000 prize for an early version of *The Many-Coloured Coat*. This is not neglect. 'The fact is', George Woodcock recently wrote in the *New Leader*, 'that Callaghan has, if anything, been overpraised in Canada, and that, if critics there were mildly annoyed at Wilson's somewhat inapt comparisons, it was not because, as he suggests, mean spirits were trying to martyr an artist, but because the time has come to look honestly at the very uneven work of a novelist who has produced some of the best Canadian writing – and also some of the worst.

I tend, for once, to agree with the Canadian point of view. I have found many of Callaghan's novels heavy going, but I think his short stories are superb and add up to the best work ever to have come out of Canada.

HUGH MACLENNAN. Canadian intellectuals are inclined to be patronizing about MacLennan because he is a culture-hero to the Canadian middle class. That is to say, those Canadians who find Yousuf Karsh artistic, CBC-TV documentaries about homosexuals thought-provoking, and the need for a Canadian theatre urgent, tend to be among MacLennan's most ardent readers. Mr. Wilson writes that MacLennan is a 'writer strongly to be recommended to anyone who wanted to understand Canada', and I would emphatically agree with this as well as the implied criticism that he can't be recommended on purely literary grounds. He can be read with enjoyment by those who look forward to the next Morris West novel or find Stanley Kramer's movies stimulating. But there is something else. MacLennan genuinely loves Canada, he worries over it, and writes about the country with intelligence and sympathy. 'He has set out', as Mr. Wilson observes, 'to render in his fiction some systematic dramatization of the life of eastern Canada.' Unfortunately, the upshot is often mechanical. MacLennan's characters seem to be fabricated of points-of-view rather than flesh and blood.

Mr. Wilson has not tried to be comprehensive, and so there is no consideration of the novels of Ethel Wilson or Robertson Davies, but what a pleasure it was to find Mavis Gallant's fiction deservedly praised for once. Mrs. Gallant, possibly because she has never run with the Can. lit. hounds, is generally overlooked in such studies. However, it is a pity that Mr. Wilson has not gone into the special relationship of the CBC to Canadian writing. For years, in the absence of literary magazines of quality, CBC radio (as distinct from CBC-TV which is largely imitative and inferior to American TV) has run a little magazine of the air, *Anthology;* and has broadcast on one programme or another the first stories, poems, plays, and criticism of our liveliest young writers. On the other hand, it was not surprising that on the first page of *O Canada* Mr. Wilson does acknowledge a debt to Robert Weaver, who was the originator of *Anthology* and is the editor of our most reputable literary magazine, *The Tamarack Review.*

Mr. Wilson notes the hostility among Canadians 'of taste (to) the ever-increasing addiction of the popular audience to (American) popular entertainments: magazines, movies, and jazz. In the case of (American) magazines, the Canadian publishers have a serious grievance that, by bringing out special Canadian editions, such periodicals as *Time* and *Reader's Digest* divert from the Canadian magazines a good part of the national advertising. . . .' All of which, I'm afraid, only adds up to a partial truth. For, as Mr. Wilson notes elsewhere, *Maclean's,* Canada's national magazine, which flourished all too briefly under Ken Lefolii's editorship, has reverted to fight its circulation battle in a sentimental quagmire abandoned by *Sat Eve Post* long ago. Other Canadian magazines are either well-intentioned but boring, like the pathetic *Canadian Forum,* or second-rate versions of American magazines, and most Canadians of taste would rather do without all Canadian magazines, than their *Statesman, Esquire, Time, New Yorker, Spectator,* or what have you. And if Canadians were shut off from American mass culture – if, as Richard Rovere once wrote, the border was sealed tight against American junk – then the country would happily set out to produce inferior junk of its own. It must also be clearly stated that the best, as well as the worst, cultural influences on Canada are American. We have always looked to New York, not Toronto, for our standards of excellence. New York is our cultural capital.

Finally, my fundamental quarrel with Mr. Wilson is he does not seem to have journeyed north so much to discover a country as to rediscover a vanished America. We Canadians, as I wrote in the *Spectator* years ago, are the English-speaking world's elected squares. To the British, we are the nicest, whitest Americans. To Americans, we represent a nostalgia for the unhurried horse and buggy age. In his youth, Mr. Wilson writes, he tended to imagine Canada as a vast hunting preserve, and even now he gets the impression in Canada of less worry and more leisure. Canadians, he feels, listen to one another, instead of 'shooting off their faces'. So it is not surprising, in this context, that Mr. Wilson found in Hugh MacLennan's book of essays, *Scotchman's Return*, 'a point of view surprisingly and agreeably different from anything else' he knew in English. Let's look at just one of the essays, *Portrait of a Year:*

> 'The year 1955 was surely one of the loveliest years any living person can remember. Like a woman of perfect tact, she let her moods follow her natural growth in harmonious sequence . . . Through January and February she was bright, flashing and thoughtless, in March she turned teenager and dumped four feet of snow on our sidewalks . . . In June she married the countryside and at once began to produce a family. . . .'

Is this so different, I wonder, from what Mr. Wilson surely would have mocked had it appeared in the *Reader's Digest?*

In *O Canada*, Mr. Wilson has justifiably accused Canadian critics of sometimes overpraising their own writers, but hasn't he, possibly in a generous mood, applied rather less severe standards to Canadian writing than he once memorably put to Somerset Maugham's work?

Having said this much, let me add that I agree with Professor Neil Compton who wrote in *Commentary* that Edmund Wilson 'wrong' still makes better reading than most critics right. And in setting out the grievances and reviewing the literature of French Canada, Mr. Wilson has written the most lucid account of a sad history for the non-specialist that I have read anywhere.

I am an obsessive reader of fringe magazines: *DOGS in Canada* (' "If people were as nice as their dogs we'd have the finest sport in the world," observed the Old Timer.'); *Police Review*, Weekly Journal of the British Police ('Ex-Supt. Arthur Williams,' begins a short story by 'Flatfoot', 'had served for thirty years in a provincial city Force and was now in retirement. He had never considered himself to be a senti-mentalist but now, each evening, seated comfortably before the television set, puffing gently on his pipe, he invariably found his mind wandering back . . .'). I also take Manchester *Jewish Life*, *Men in Vogue*, *Toronto Life* ('As winter-time became ensconced in Toronto, party began to follow party. . . .'), and many, many more. But in 1967, in the months before I planned to return to Canada for the first time in three years, the magazine that afforded me the most pleasure was *the stage in Canada*, published monthly by the Canadian Theatre Centre in Toronto. The January issue, vintage stuff, featured the report of the Theatre Centre's professional ethics committee, a group that met under the chairmanship of one Malcolm Black. Among the ten articles in the pro-posed code of ethics, the ones I found the most stirring were:

2. *Observe the Golden Rule:* . . . Members ought to treat each other as they prefer to be treated. Members ought to *observe the golden rule.*

7. *Enhance the professional image:* Whether or not we of the Theatre continue to be viewed as 'rogues and vagabonds' depends on us, and our sincere attempts to *enhance our professional image.*

10. *Use imagination:* As artists, we include imagination as part of our stock-in-trade . . . Members are urged, at all times, in all situations, to *use imagination.*

Canada, Canada. Older than Bertrand Russell. A hundred years old in 1967. 'A nation like no other,' begins the Centennial Library brochure, 'larger than the entire continent of Europe, second in size only to Russia . . . Canada is unique.'

IN MONTREAL, I read in the New York *Times*, COMPLETE ASSURANCE SPEAKS IN 2 LANGUAGES. Mrs. Charles Taschereau told the *Times* that she found it difficult to keep still. 'If I have nothing else to do,' she said, 'I might paint a wall.' Mrs. Hartland Molson described my Montreal as a city of 'living within the home,' except for hockey games and visiting friends, whilst Mrs. Samuel Bronfman said, 'I love people, but my husband is a better judge of them.' Such nice, simple people, the Canadian rich, but I found the new personalities and events baffling. On arrival, for instance, what should my attitude be toward Judy LaMarsh, the minister responsible for culture? Who was Peter Reilly? What was psychedelic TV? I wished EXPO the best, the very best, but where were they going to find enough fellow-travellers to fill the Expo Theatre for The Popular Stars of Prague on September 1st? Hungering for more information about home, I devoured the Canadian magazines, especially the intellectual ones, like *The Canadian Forum*. One month I read, 'In 1965, 73,980 Canadians died of heart disease, 63,000 were seriously or totally crippled by arthritis, and 25,637 died of cancer. There were 670 who died of TB, half of them people over 70 years of age.' I commit this to memory, my experience of the world has been enriched. Another month I read in the same puzzling magazine, 'The 19 Supreme and County Court rooms in Toronto's new courthouse have been panelled in teak from Burma and Siam, mahogany from Africa and Honduras, oak and walnut from the U.S. and English oak. No Canadian panelling was used.'

Was this, I wondered, a snippet of dialogue from a new Harold Pinter play? No. It was hard fact. Meant to make me angry, I suppose. After all, why all that snobbish British oak and warmongering American walnut in our courthouses? Was Canadian wood wormy or something?

The truth was, I decided, weeks before leaving for Montreal, I no longer understood the idiom. Doomed to always be a foreigner in England, I was now in danger of finding Canada foreign too. After thirteen almost uninterrupted years abroad, I now realized the move I had made with such certainty at the age of twenty-three had exacted a considerable price. Some foggy, depressing nights it seemed to me that I had come full circle. Many years ago my parents emigrated from Poland to Canada, to Montreal, where I grew up ashamed of their Yiddish accents. Now I had seemingly settled in London, where my own children (spoiled, ungrateful, enjoying an easier childhood than I had, etc. etc.) found my American accent just as embarrassing.

Still, being a Canadian writer abroad offers a writer a number of built-in perks. I have, through the years, been turning over a useful penny in the why-have-you-left-Canada interview, that is to say, once a year I make a fool of myself on TV for a fee.

Most recently a breathless girl from Toronto sat in my garden, crossed her legs distractingly as the TV cameras turned, smiled cutely, and said, 'I've never read anything you've written but would you say you were part of the brain-drain?'

Sure, baby. I also assure her that I'm an Angry Young Man. A black humorist. A white Negro. Anything.

'But why did you leave Canada in the first place?'

I daren't tell her that I had no girl friends. That having been born dirty-minded I had thought in London maybe, in Paris certainly, the girls. . . . Instead, I say, 'Well, it was a cultural desert, wasn't it? In London, I could see the Sadlers Wells Ballet, plays by Terence Rattigan. If overcome with a need to see the Popular Stars of Prague, I could hop on

27

a plane and jolly well see them. *In their natural environment.*

I arrived in Montreal late in June.

'QUEEN LEADS CELEBRATIONS,' ran the July 1st headline in the Montreal *Star*. 'Canada is 100 years young today and Queen Elizabeth is doing her royal best to make it a real blast.' Dominion Day, Prime Minister Pearson declared handsomely, belonged to all of us. 'Every one of you, and every Canadian before you, has had some part, however humble and unsung, in building the magnificent structure that we honour and salute today.'

Mr. Pearson, once feared to be an intellectual, showed himself a most regular (dare I say all-American?) guy in a recent interview with *Macleans*. Asked who was the greatest man he had ever met, he replied: 'If you mean the man – leaving my father out – who made the greatest impression on me personally, it would be Mr. Downey, a teacher in my public school in Peterborough, when I was a boy.'

'Can you recall anything that you're now ashamed of?'

'Considering that I've lived 70 years, I have a reasonable immunity from guilt. But I certainly have done some things I later regretted. I cheated in geography class once when I was in Grade 6 or 7, I think, and I've never forgotten it.'

Canadians, notably reticent in the past, flooded the Dominion Day newspapers with self-congratulatory ads. Typical was the full page run by Eaton's, our largest department store chain, which asked, 'WHO ARE YOU, CANADA?' Roaring back came the unastonishing answer, '. . . the young giant. The young giant of the North. . . .' Without a doubt, the most imaginative of the Dominion Day ads began:

A GROWING NATION . . .

A GROWING PROFESSION . . .

A GROWING FIRM . . .

In just 100 years, our nation has grown to assume a leading position in the world . . . a position of which all

Canadians can be justifiably proud as we observe our Centennial.

Canadian funeral service has grown, too, always keeping in step with changing times . . . And at D.A. Collins Funeral Homes, where we've been serving for 54 out of Canada's 100 years, progress . . .

Canada, 98 years without a flag, went so far as to commission a Toronto ad agency to produce a Centennial song. 'What we needed', an executive vice-president of the agency told a reporter, 'was a grabber. A stirring flag-waver that would make everybody feel, "Gee, this is a real good country." ' Bobby Gimby, a radio jingle writer, came up with the grabber which has been a fantastic success.

CA-NA-DA

(One little two little three Canadians)

WE LOVE THEE

(Now we are twenty million)

CA-NA-DA

(Four little five little six little Provinces)

PROUD AND FREE

(Now we are ten and the Territories – sea to sea)

North, South, East, West

There'll be happy times

Church bells will ring, ring, ring

It's the hundredth anniversary of

Con-fed-er-a-tion

Ev'-ry-bo-dy sing, to-geth-er

CA-NA-DA

(Un petit deux petit trois Canadiens)

NOTRE PAY-EE (Pays)

(Maintenant nous sommes vingt millions)

CA-NA-DA

(Quatre petites cinq petites six petites Provinces)

LON-GUE VIE
(Et nous sommes dix plus les Territoires – Lon-gue vie)
Hur-rah! Vive le Canada!
Three cheers, hip, hip, hooray!
Le Centenaire!
That's the order of the day
Frère Jacques, Frère Jacques
Merrily we roll along
To-geth-er, all the way.

1967 being our big year, there was a tendency to measure all things Canadian, and so the Canadian Authors' Association sent out a questionnaire to writers asking, among other things,

> What contemporary prose writer(s) has the best chance of still being read in 2000 A.D.?..
> How many words a year do you write?..
> How many words a year do you sell?..
> As a writer what do you most often wish for: inspiration, ideas, better research facilities, an agent, a public relations man, more markets, higher royalties, a grant, more hours to write, etc...
> *Note:* Please answer only in terms of the Canadian scene in all questions – whether specified or not.

Enclosed was a copy of *The Canadian Author and Bookman*, the Association's quarterly, in which I found an ad for *Yarns of the Yukon*, by Herman G. Swerdloff, with rave reviews from *Alaska Highway News* and *R.C.M.P. Quarterly;* and a critical study of Margaret Lawrence (*The Stone Angel, A Jest Of God*) that began 'Margaret (Wemyss) Lawrence was born with a pen in her hand and a story in her heart.' There was also a double page spread of poems by expatriates with the corporate title HELLO CANADA. One of the poems was 'from homesick Maggie Dominic in New York,' who wrote 'This year, 1966, as prompted by Premier Joseph R. Smallwood, is Come Home Newfoundlander Year. Being a Newfoundlander and a writer, I was asked to compose a poem, commemorating c.h.y./66 for Newfoundland . . . I have been published in the United States, Canada, and most recently India.'

The c.a.a. not only held its 1967 conference at Expo, but also summoned a Congress of Universal Writers to 'deal definitively with the role of the author (creator of fiction, interpreter of universal truth, ambassador of good-will, agitator, reformer, propagandist, inventor of language, etc. . . .).' The u.s.s.r. sent Alexander Chakovsky, editor of the *Literary Gazette*, and the *Reader's Digest* (Canada) Ltd. shipped us James Michener. Already gathered in Montreal were such Canadian writers as Bluebell Phillips, Phoebe Erskine Hyde, Fanny Shulman, Grace Scrimgeour, Una Wardelworth, and Madeline Kent de Espinosa. Opening night, there was a party for Universal Writers, but though it was sponsored by the largest of Canadian distilleries, Seagram's, nothing more potent than coffee was served. At the meeting following the party, a friend reported, the ladies stood up one by one to announce how their branch regional histories were going. It was all very dull, my friend said, until suddenly, one lady rose to announce *she* had just finished a book called *Ripe and Ready*. As things turned out, the lady had not, to quote the *Bookman*, 'prostituted her talent by writing sex-dripping prose.' *Ripe And Ready* was in fact a history of apples.

'It's just great to be a Canadian this year,' as John David Hamilton wrote in the *New Statesman*. 'It's as if we suddenly turned on, in the hippie sense, when our hundredth birthday arrived. . . . At any rate, we are in the midst of an earthquake of national pride – for the first time in our history.' Yes; and the quake has yielded a mountain of non-books, from the reasonably priced *Life* library-like Canadian Centennial Library

(*Great Canadians*, *Great Canadian Writing*, *Great Canadian Sports Stories*, etc.), through a Beginning Reader's McGraw-Hill series on the 10 provinces, to the over-priced and exceedingly pretentious *To Everything There Is A Season*, a picture book by Roloff Beny (The Viking Press, $25). Mr. Beny introduces his book, somewhat grandiosely, with a quotation from Herman Hesse. 'He looked around him as if seeing the world for the first time. . . .' And yet, *To Everything There Is A Season*, like all picture books I've seen on Canada, as well as many an old calendar, manages to contain all the clichés, albeit 'poetically' seen. There is, for instance, the photograph of the age-old rocks beaten into egg-shape by the timeless sea; we are given the essential snow-shrouded tree; the ripe and ready apples rotting on the ground; the obligatory field of wild flowers; the autumnal woods; the Quebec churches etc. etc. etc. The truth is that though Mr. Beny is by trade a photographer, it is his prose style that singles his volume out for special interest. Comparing himself to a contemporary Ulysses, allowing that his collection of photographs is both 'retrospective and prophetic', he writes that his was a personal odyssey, a voyage of discovery and rediscovery. Mr. Beny came to Canada via 'Olympian heights', risking 'the *son et lumière* of Wagnerian thunderstorms', which is to say, like most of us, he flew. His findings however were singular. '. . . the serene stretches of the St. Lawrence recalled the sacred Ganges; the South Saskatchewan . . . was the Tague River which loops the fabled city of El Greco – Toledo . . . Ottawa, its Gothic silhouette reflected in the river, was Mont Saint Michel . . . and Calgary . . . was Teheran, which boasts the same cool, dry climate and poplar trees.'

The last time I was in Montreal, my home town, was in 1964. 'Québec Libre' was freshly painted on many a wall, and students were fixing stickers that read 'Québec Oui Ottawa Non' on car windows. Militant French-Canadian Separatism, and not Expo, was the talking point. I had returned to Montreal, as I wrote in *Encounter* at the time, on Queen Victoria's birthday, a national holiday in Canada. A thousand policemen were required to put down a French-Canadian Separatist demonstration. Flags were burnt, a defective bomb was planted on Victoria Bridge, and a wreath was laid at the *Monument aux Patriots* which marks the spot where twelve men were executed after the 1837-38 rebellion. The city was feverish. André Laurendeau, then editor of *Le Devoir*, developed the popular theory of 'Roi Nègre,' that is to say that the real rulers of Quebec (the English, represented by the Federal Government in Ottawa) used a French-Canadian chieftain (former, and once all powerful, Provincial Premier Duplessis) to govern the French, just as colonial powers used African puppets to keep their tribes in order. André Malraux, in town to open a 'France in Canada' exhibition, told the City Council, 'France needs you. We will build the next civilization together.' Malraux added that he had brought a personal message from General de Gaulle. It was that 'Montreal was France's second city. He wanted this message to reach you. . . . You are not aware of the meaning you have for France. There is nowhere in the world where the spirit of France works so movingly as it does in the province of Quebec.'

Naturally, this made for an uproar, so that the next day at a hastily summoned press conference Malraux said, 'The mere thought that French Canada could become politically or otherwise dependent on France is a dangerous and even ridiculous one.'

Since then, as we all know, De Gaulle himself has been and gone, shouting the Separatist slogan, 'Vive le Québec libre!' from the balcony of Montreal City Hall, and Prime Minister Pearson, rising to the occasion for once, declared that this was 'unacceptable' to the Canadian Government. I doubt that De Gaulle's outburst, enjoyable as it was to *all*

33

French Canadians, will make more than a momentary Separatist resurgence, but it is worth noting that France has not always been so enamoured of Quebec, a province which was largely pro-Vichy in sentiment during the war, and whose flag is still the fleur-de-lis.

In the summer of 1964, André d'Allemagne, one of the leaders of the RIN (*Le Parti Républicain du Québec*) told me that in his struggle for an independent state of Quebec he was opposed to violence, but, should his party be outlawed, he might be obliged to turn to it. 'Like the *maquis*.' D'Allemagne looked to the next Quebec provincial election in 1966 as the big test – and he wasn't the only one.

But, in 1966, the RIN which claimed 8,500 militant members, failed to win a seat. Quebec, to almost everyone's astonishment, veered to the right again. Jean Lesage's reform Liberal Government, which worked fairly well with Lester Pearson's Federal Government, also Liberal, was squeezed out and the *Union Nationale*, the late Maurice Duplessis's graft-ridden toy for so many years, was returned, with a majority of two, under Daniel Johnson, largely because Lesage was moving too quickly for the backwoods villages and townships.

This summer I returned to Montreal in time for the St. Jean Baptiste parade on June 23. St. Jean Baptiste is the patron saint of Quebec. In 1964, for the first time, he was no longer played by a boy in the annual parade. Instead, he was represented by an adult, and the sheep that had accompanied him in former years was tossed out. This summer's St. Jean Baptiste parade was a dull, tepid affair. Minor officials and French-Canadian *vedettes* riding in open cars were followed by a seemingly endless run of unimaginative floats. Certainly the mood a week before De Gaulle's visit was not one to make for double-locks in Westmount Mansions, where Montreal's richest WASPS live. If only three years ago English-speaking Canadians were running scared, then this summer, whenever the so-called 'Quiet Revolution' came up, it was as a joke. 'Have you heard the one about the Pepsi (French Canadian), watching hockey on TV, who lost a hundred dollars on a Toronto goal against Montreal?' 'No.' 'He lost fifty dollars on the goal. And another fifty on the replay.' (The replay being the instant TV re-run of the goal just scored.)

In the early Sixties, French Canadians justifiably complained that while it was necessary for them to speak fluent English to qualify for most jobs, English-speaking Canadians were not obliged to know French. English Canada's haste to remedy this imbalance by hiring French Canadians, sometimes indiscriminately, has spawned another joke. A man sitting by a pool sees a lady drowning. 'Help, help,' she cries. The man rushes over to the French-Canadian lifeguard and shouts, 'Aren't you going to do anything?' 'I can't swim,' he says. 'What! You're a lifeguard and you can't swim?' 'I don't have to. I'm bilingual.'

Then newly elected Quebec Premier Daniel Johnson, eager to demonstrate that he is his people's champion, has put through a decree that will make the use of French obligatory in all inscriptions of packaged foods and tins . . . which has led to speculation among Jews about the labels on next year's matzohs.

Montreal has always seemed to me an unusually handsome and lively city, but in recent months the mounting hyperbole in Expo-inspired articles in American and British publications had made me apprehensive. A case in point is the London *Sunday Times*, whose colour supplement on Canada included a piece with the title, 'Montreal: Canada's Answer to Paris, London and New York.' In the same issue, Penelope Mortimer, back from a flying trip to Montreal, wrote that she had just been able 'to observe the customs of some of the most lively, uninhibited, civilized, humane, and adventurous people in the world today – the Canadians. . . .' I also had serious doubts about Expo itself. If it was ludicrous but somehow touching that Canada, after ninety-eight years and an endlessly embarrassing debate in Ottawa, had voted itself a flag, it seemed exceedingly late in the day to bet 800 million dollars on so unsophisticated an idea as a world's fair dedicated to the theme of 'Man and His World' (*Terres des Hommes*). Let me say at once, then, that Expo is, as they say, awfully good fun and in the best possible taste.

Even more impressive to an old Montrealer, perhaps, are the changes that Expo has wrought on the city itself. On earlier visits to Montreal, during the past twelve years, I was asked again and again if I could 'recognize' the city, and of course I always could. But this time, after an absence of only three years, I was in fact overwhelmed by the difference. Suddenly, all the ambitious building of twelve years, the high-rise apartments, the downtown skyscrapers, the slum clearance projects, the elegant new metro, the Place Ville Marie, the Place des Arts, the new network of express highways, the new hotels, have added up to another city. If, for many years, the choice open to me (and other Canadian writers, painters, and film-makers living abroad) was whether to suffer home or remain an expatriate, the truth quite simply is that the choice no longer exists. Home has been pulverized, bull-dozed and spilled into the St. Lawrence to create an artificial island: Isle Notre-Dame. Home, suddenly, is terrifyingly affluent. Montreal is the richest-looking city I've seen in years.

Many of the new skycrapers, it's true, are of the familiar biscuit-box variety, but there has also been a heartening drive to restore the old quarter, Bonsecours Market, the narrow cobblestone streets that surround it, and the baroque City Hall. The antique market is booming. Montreal even publishes its very own fervent right-wing magazine, *Canada Month*. In the most recent issue, Irving Layton, the country's best known 'most outspoken, exuberant and controversial' poet, came out for American policy in Vietnam. 'I think the Americans are fighting this war, not because they want to overthrow Chinese communism, or for that matter, even the communism of Uncle Ho-Ho'; rather, he felt, America's sole interest was its own territorial security.

I've been in Montreal twice this year: the first time just a week before Expo opened, and it was then that I first visited the American pavilion, Buckminster Fuller's transparent geodesic sphere, which is still, to my mind, the most fascinating structure at Expo. The sphere, 20 stories high, 250 feet in diameter, the plastic skin held together by a network of triangulated aluminium tubes, is a delight to the eye seen from any angle, inside or out; and in fact dominates the Expo grounds. The lighthearted stuff on display inside had been severely criticized by the time I visited the sphere a second time, late in June, and the PR man who escorted me explained: 'We try to tell all our colleagues in the media that this is not an exhibition. It's only meant to show the spirit symbolic of – well, you know.'

Camp, he might have said. There are enormous stills of vintage Hollywood stars (Bogart, Gable, Joan Crawford) and a screen that runs great scenes from past movies, such as the chariot race from *Ben Hur*. On the next floor there is a display of pop art (Dine, Lichtenstein, Johns, Warhol), some pictures running as much as ten stories high. The highest floor is taken up with the inevitable display of spacecraft and paraphernalia. Briefly, it is the softest of all possible sells, radiating self-confidence.

The chunky British pavilion, designed by Sir Basil Spence is meant to be self-mocking, and so it is, sometimes unintentionally. Embossed in concrete on an outside wall stands 'BRITAIN,' pointedly without the 'GREAT,' though the French inscription reads 'GRANDE BRETAGNE.' Inside, the glossy scenes of contemporary British life suggest what Malcolm

Muggeridge has called Sunday Supplement living taken into the third dimension. The pretty hostesses, as I'm sure you've read elsewhere, are mini-skirted and carry Union Jack handbags. If the declared theme is 'The Challenge of Change' then, endearingly, it reveals how this challenge has been met. Wall charts of British geniuses list numbered photographs (Dickens, 12; Turner, 82), and before each chart there stands a computer. Theoretically, one should be able to press a number on the computer and come up with a card crammed with information. In practice, at Expo as in contemporary Britain itself, all the computers were marked TEMPORARILY OUT OF ORDER.

With other, larger powers usurping Canada's traditional self-effacing stance, it has fallen on the host nation to play it straight. Outside the Canadian pavilion there is a decidedly non-joke mountie on horseback, a sitting duck for camera-laden tourists in Bermuda shorts, who pose their children before him endlessly. Nearby stands Canada's People Tree. 'As its name implies, the People Tree symbolizes the people of Canada. A stylized maple soaring to a height of 66 feet . . . it reflects the personal, occupational, and recreational activities of more than 20 million individuals. . . .' Briefly, a multi-coloured, illuminated magazine cover tree.

At the Tundra, the Canadian pavilion restaurant, it is possible to order Buffalo bouchées or whale steak. Robert Fulford of the Toronto *Star* has written that if the pavilion bar were really to represent Canada it would have to be 'a pit of Muzak-drenched darkness . . . or, perhaps one of those sour-smelling enamel rooms in which waiters, wearing change aprons, slop glasses of draught beer all over the tables and patrons.' Instead, it is well-lit and handsomely designed, with authentic Eskimo murals.

The most truculent of the pavilions is the small one representing embattled Cuba, plastered with photographs of the revolution and headlines that run to ATOMIC BLACKMAIL, DEATH, LSD, CIA, NAPALM. Outside the Czech pavilion, the most popular at Expo, the queues wind round and round, whole families waiting submissively in the sun for two, sometimes three, hours. Actually, none of the pavilion interiors is so gratifying as the gay Expo site itself, where I spent my most exhilarating hours simply strolling about. The improbable, even zany, pavilions are such a welcome change from the urban landscape we are all accustomed to: there are almost no cars, and the streets are astonishingly clean and quiet. Expo, only ten minutes from downtown Montreal by road or metro, lies on the island of Montreal proper, St. Helen's Island, and the artificially created island of Notre-Dame. In the early forties, when I was a boy in Montreal, St. Helen's Island was the untamed and gritty place to which working-class kids escaped for picnics and swims on sweltering summer days. There was, and still is, an old fort on the island. In 1940, Mayor Camillien Houde, a corrupt but engaging French-Canadian politician of Louisiana dimensions, was briefly interned there for advising young French Canadians not to register for conscription in a British imperialist war. Houde's companions included communists, also rounded up by the RCMP, and baffled Jewish-German refugees, sent over from England where they had been classified as enemy aliens. Now the island is tricked out with lagoons, fountains, canals, and artificial lakes.

In the months before Expo opened, probably no individual structure was more highly publicized than Habitat 67, Moshe Safdie's prefabricated design for cheap, high-density housing, the novelty being that the roof of one apartment would serve as the garden terrace of another, and that the entire unit, looking rather like a haphazard pile of children's blocks, could be assembled by a crane slipped into place alongside. Without a doubt, this angular concrete block has no place in Montreal with its long and bitter winters. Habitat

67, projecting out of a green hill in a tropical climate, could be something else again.

In any event, I think Expo is more likely to be remembered for its films rather than any particular building, save Buckminster Fuller's geodesic sphere. Films charge at you everywhere, from multiple and wrap-around screens, bounced off floors, stone walls, mirrors, and what-not. Alas, the pyrotechnics, the dazzling techniques, conceal, for the most part, nothing more than old-fashioned documentaries about life in Ontario, Czechoslovakia, Mod England, etc. The most highly touted and ambitious of these films, the Canadian National Film Board's *Labyrinth*, is also the most popular individual exhibit at Expo, its queues waiting as long as four hours.

Produced by Roman Kroiter, an undoubtedly talented filmmaker, housed in a specially constructed building, *Labyrinth* took more than two years and four and a half million dollars to make. Based on the legend of the Minotaur, *Labyrinth* is actually two films. The first, seen from multi-levelled galleries, is projected on two whopping big screens: one on a wall, the other on a sunken floor bed. At its most successful, it is tricky (child seen on wall screen throws a pebble *which lands with a splash* in a pool on floor screen) or aims at creating vertigo (suddenly, we are looking straight down a missile chute). From here, viewers grope their way through a spookhouse type maze into a multi-screened theatre, wherein we learn that man comes into this world bloody and wailing and leaves in a coffin. Unfortunately, in this case it would seem that it is life that is long and art that's short. En route to the grave, we are instructed that all men are brothers (black, white, and yellow men, popping to life, simultaneously on the multi-screen) and are treated to an occasional brilliant sequence such as the crocodile hunt. But two years in the making, four and a half million dollars spent ... the return seems both portentous and inadequate.

Finally Expo has done more for Canada's self-confidence than anything within memory. 'By God, we did it! And generally we did it well,' Pierre Berton wrote in *Macleans*.

'We're on the map,' a friend told me. 'They know who we are in New York now.'

Hugo McPherson, professor of Canadian and American studies at the University of Western Ontario until recently and now head of the National Film Board, said in an interview: 'We have our own "scene" in Canada now. . . . It's no longer fashionable, the way it used to be, for Canadians to knock everything Canadian. Perhaps Expo will be the event we'll all remember as the roadmark. I think it's going to be a vast Canadianizing force, not only in Quebec but all across the country. There's a new feeling of national gaiety and pride at Expo. . . .'

Others go even further, demanding an alarmingly high emotional return from what is after all only a world's fair. A good one, maybe even the most enjoyable one ever. However, within it there lies merely the stuff of a future nostalgic musical, not the myth out of which a nation is forged. Unless it is to be a Good Taste Disneyland.

In 1963 the world ice hockey championships were not only
held in Stockholm but, for the third time, the Swedes were
the incumbent champions and the team to beat. Other
threatening contenders were the Czechs and the Russians,
and the team everyone had come to see humiliated was our
own peppery but far from incomparable Trail Smoke Eaters.

'No nations can form ties of friendship without there
being personal contact between the peoples. In these respects
sports builds on principles of long standing,' Helge Berglund,
president of the Swedish Hockey Association, wrote warmly
in the world hockey tournament's 1963 programme. Berglund's bubbly letter of greeting continued, 'I do hope the
ice hockey players will feel at home here and that you will
take advantage of your leisure to study Swedish culture and
Swedish life. Welcome to our country.'

Yes indeed; but on the day I arrived in Stockholm a poster
advertising a sports magazine on kiosks everywhere an-
nounced THE CANADIANS WANT TO SEE BLOOD.
Only a few days later a headline in the Toronto Star read
UGLY ROW IN SWEDEN OVER OUR HOCKEY
TEAM.

I checked into the Hotel Continental, a well-lit teak-
ridden place where well on a hundred other reporters, radio
and television men, referees, a hockey priest, and a contin-
gent of twenty-seven Russians, were staying; and immediately sought out Jim Proudfoot of the Toronto *Star*.
Proudfoot had just returned from a cocktail party at the
Canadian embassy. 'What did the players have to say?' I
asked.

'The players weren't invited.'

The next morning things began to sizzle. On Saturday night, according to the most colourful Swedish newspapers, a substitute player with the Canadian team, Russ Kowalchuk, tried to smuggle a girl into his room and was knocked senseless by an outraged hall porter. Kowalchuk, enthusiastically described as a 'star' in one Swedish newspaper and 'a philandering hoodlum' in another, was not flattered: he denied that there had been a girl involved in the incident and claimed he had been flattened by a sneak punch.

Two things worried me about this essentially commonplace story. While it seemed credible that a hotel porter might be shocked if a hockey player tried to sneak a stuffed rabbit into the elevator, it did seem absurd that he would be shaken to his roots if a man, invited by Helge Berglund to study Swedish life, tried to take a girl to his room. And if the Canadians were such a rough-and-ready lot, if they were determined to crush Swedish bones in Friday night's game, wasn't it deflating that one of their defencemen could be knocked out by a mere porter? More important, mightn't it even hurt the gate?

The Trail Smoke Eaters, as well as the Czech, Russian, and American players, were staying at the Malmen – not, to put it mildly, the most elegant of hotels, a feeling, I might add, obviously shared by the amateur hockey officials associated with the Smoke Eaters, which group sagaciously put up at the much more commodious Grand Hotel.

When I finally got to the Malmen at noon on Sunday I found the side-walk outside all but impassable. Kids clutching autograph books, older boys in black leather jackets, and fetching girls who didn't look like they'd need much encouragement to come in out of the cold, jostled each other by the entrance. An American player emerged from the hotel and was quickly engulfed by a group of autograph-hungry kids. 'Shove off,' he said, leading with his elbows; and if the kids (who, incidentally, learn to speak three languages at school) didn't grasp the colloquialism immediately then the player's message, I must say, was implicit in his tone. The kids scattered. The American player, however, stopped a little further down the street for three girls and signed his name for them. I knew he *could* sign too, for, unlike the amateurs of other nations, he was neither a reinstated pro, army officer or sports equipment manufacturer, but a bona fide student. Possibly, he could sign *very well*.

In the lobby of the Malmen, Bobby Kromm, the truculent coach of the Smoke Eaters, was shouting at a Swedish journalist. Other players, reporters, camp followers, cops, *agents provocateurs*, and strong-armed hotel staff milled about, seemingly bored. Outside, kids with their noses flattened against the windows tried to attract the attention of the players who slouched in leather chairs. Suddenly the Russian team, off to a game, emerged from the elevators, already in playing uniforms and carrying sticks. A Canadian journalist whispered to me, 'Don't they look sinister?' As a matter of fact, if you overlooked the absence of facial stitches, they closely resembled the many Canadians of Ukrainian origin who play in the National Hockey League.

Bobby Kromm and his assistant manager, Don Freer, were also off to the game, but they agreed to meet me at eight o'clock.

When I returned to the Malmen that evening I saw a car parked by the entrance, three girls waiting in the back seat. Kids, also hoping to attract the players' attention, were banging pennies against the lobby windows. The players ignored them, sucking on matchsticks. Kromm, Freer and I went into the dining room, and while I ordered a cognac I was gratified to see that the reputedly terrifying Smoke Eaters, those behemoths who struck fear into the hearts of both Swedish mothers and Russian defencemen, stuck to coffee and pie.

Kromm, assuming our elderly waiter could understand

English, barked his order at him and was somewhat put out – in fact he complained in a voice trained to carry out to centre ice – when the waiter got his order wrong. The waiter began to mutter. 'You see,' Kromm said, 'they just don't like Canadians here.'

I nodded sympathetically.

'Why do they serve us pork chops, *cold* pork chops, for *breakfast?*'

'If you don't like it here, why don't you check out and move right into another hotel?'

This wasn't possible, Kromm explained. Their stay at the Malmen was prepaid. It had been arranged by John Ahearne, European president of the International Ice Hockey Federation, who, as it turned out, also ran a travel agency. 'If they treat us good here', Kromm said, 'we'd treat them good.'

Freer explained that the Smoke Eaters had nothing against the Swedes, but they felt the press had used them badly.

'They called me a slum,' Kromm said, 'Am I a slum?'

'No. But what,' I asked, 'is your big complaint here?'

Bobby Kromm pondered briefly. 'We've got nothing to do at night. Why couldn't they give us a ping-pong table?'

Were these men the terror of Stockholm? On the contrary. It seemed to me they would have delighted the heart of any YMCA athletic director. Freer told me proudly that nine of the twenty-one players on the team had been born and raised in Trail and that ten of them worked for the C.M. and S.

'What does that stand for?' I asked.

'I dunno,' he said.

It stands for Consolidated Mining & Smelting, and Bobby Kromm is employed as a glass blower by the company. All of them would be compensated for lost pay.

Kromm said, 'We can't step out of the hotel without feeling like monkeys in a cage. People point you out on the streets and laugh.'

'It might help if you didn't wear those blazing red coats everywhere.'

'We haven't any other coats.'

I asked Kromm why European players didn't go in for body-checking.

'They condone it,' he said, 'that's why.'

I must have looked baffled.

'They condone it. Don't you understand?'

I did, once I remembered that when Kromm had been asked by another reporter for his version of the girl-in-the-lobby incident, he had said, 'O.K., I'll give you my impersonation of it.'

Kromm and Freer were clear about one thing. 'We'd never come back here again.'

Jackie McLeod, the only player on the team with National Hockey League experience, didn't want to come back again either. I asked him if he had, as reported, been awakened by hostile telephone calls. He had been wakened, he said, but the calls weren't hostile. 'Just guys in nightclubs wanting us to come out and have a drink with them.'

While Canadian and Swedish journalists were outraged by Kowalchuk's misadventures the men representing international news agencies found the tournament dull and Stockholm a sub-zero and most expensive bore. Late every night the weary reporters, many of whom had sat through three hockey games a day in a cold arena, gathered in the makeshift press club at the Hotel Continental. Genuine melancholy usually set in at two a.m.

'If only we could get one of the Russian players to defect.'

'You crazy? To work for a lousy smelting factory in Trail? Those guys have it really good, you know.'

The lowest paid of all the amateurs were the Americans, who were given twenty dollars spending money for the entire European tour; and the best off, individually, was undoubtedly the Swedish star, Tumba Johansson. Tumba, a ten-dollar-a-game amateur, had turned down a Boston Bruin contract offer but not, I feel, because he was intent on keeping his status pure. A national hero, Tumba earns a reputed forty thousand dollars a year through a hockey equipment manufacturer. First night on the ice not many Swedish players wore helmets. 'Don't worry,' a local reporter said, 'they'll be wearing their helmets for Tumba on Wednesday. Wednesday they're on TV'.

It was most exhilarating to be a Canadian in Stockholm. Everywhere else I've been in Europe I've generally had to explain where and what Canada was, that I was neither quite an American nor really a colonial. But in Sweden there was no need to fumble or apologize. Canadians are known, widely known, and widely disliked. It gave me a charge, this – a real charge – as if I actually came from a country important enough to be feared.

The affable Helge Berglund, president of the Swedish Ice Hockey Association, claims there are more than a hundred thousand active players and about seven thousand hockey teams in Sweden. How fitting, he reflects, that the Johanneshov *isstadion* should be the scene of the world championship competition. 'The stadium's fame as the Mecca of ice hockey', he continues in his own bouncy style, 'is once more sustained.'

My trouble was I couldn't get into Mecca.

'You say that you have just come from London for the *Macleans*,' the official said warily, 'but how do I know you are not a . . . chancer?'

With the help of the Canadian embassy I was able to establish that I was an honest reporter.

'I could tell you were not a chancer,' the official said, smiling now, 'a man doesn't flow all the way from London just for a free ticket.'

'You're very perceptive,' I said.

'They think here I am a fool that I do everybody favours – even the Russians. But if I now go to Moscow they do me a favour and if I come to London,' he said menacingly, 'you are happy to do me a favour too.'

Inside the *isstadion*, the Finns were playing the West Germans. A sloppy, lacklustre affair. Very little bodily contact. If a Finn and a West German collided they didn't exactly say excuse me: neither did any of them come on in rough National League style.

I returned the same night, Monday, to watch the Smoke Eaters play the exhausted, dispirited Americans. Down four goals to begin with, the Canadians easily rallied to win ten to four. The game, a dull one, was not altogether uninstructive. I had been placed in the press section and in the seats below me agitated agency men, reporters from Associated Press, United Press International, Canadian Press, and other news organizations, sat with pads on their knees and telephones clapped to their ears. There was a scramble round the American nets and a goal was scored.

'Em, it looked like number ten to me,' one of the agency men ventured.

'No – no – it was number six.'

'Are you sure?'

'Absolutely.'

'I'm with Harry,' the man from another agency said. 'I think it was number ten.'

A troubled pause.

'Maybe we ought to wait for the official scorer?'

'Tell you what, as long as we all agree it was number ten –'

'Done.'

All at once, the agency men began to talk urgently into their telephones.

'. . . and the Smoke Eaters add yet another tally. The second counter of the series for. . . .'

The next game I saw – Canada vs. Czechoslovakia – was what the sporting writers of my Montreal boyhood used to call the big one, a four-pointer. Whoever lost this one was unlikely to emerge world champion. Sensing the excitement, maybe even hoping for a show of violence, some fifteen thousand people turned up for the match. Most of them were obliged to stand for the entire game, maybe two hours.

This was an exciting contest, the lead seesawing back and forth throughout. The Czech amateurs are not only better paid than ours, but play with infinitely more elegance. Superb stick-handlers and accurate passers, they skated circles round the Smoke Eaters, overlooking only one thing: in order to score frequently it is necessary to shoot on the nets. While the Czechs seemed loath to part with the puck the more primitive Canadians couldn't get rid of it quickly enough. Their approach was to wind up and belt the puck in the general direction of the Czech zone, all five players digging in after it.

The spectators – except for one hoarse and lonely voice that seemed to come from the farthest reaches of Helge Berglund's Mecca – delighted in every Canadian pratfall. From time to time the isolated Canadian supporter called out in a mournful voice, 'Come on, Canada.'

The Czechs had a built-in cheering section behind their bench. Each time one of their players put stick and puck together a banner was unfurled and at least a hundred chunky broadshouldered men began to leap up and down and shout something that sounded like, 'Umpa-Umpa-Czechoslo-vakia!'

Whenever a Czech player scored, their bench would empty, everybody spilling out on the ice to embrace, leap in the air, and shout joyously. The Canadian team, made of cooler stuff, would confine their scoring celebration to players already out on the ice. With admirable unselfconsciousness,

I thought, the boys would skate up and down poking each other on the behind with their hockey sticks.

The game, incidentally, ended in a four-four tie.

The Canadians wanted to see blood, the posters said. Hoodlums, one newspaper said. The red jackets go hunting at night, another claimed. George Gross, the Toronto *Telegram's* outraged reporter, wrote, 'Anti-Canadian feeling is so strong here it has become impossible to wear a maple leaf on your lapel without being branded ruffian, hooligan and – since yesterday – sex maniac.'

A man, that is to say, a Canadian man, couldn't help but walk taller in such a heady atmosphere, absorbing some of the fabled Smoke Eaters' virility by osmosis. But I must confess that no window shutters were drawn as I walked down the streets. Mothers did not lock up their daughters. I was not called ruffian, hooligan, or anything even mildly deprecating. Possibly, the trouble was I wore no maple leaf in my lapel.

Anyway, in the end everything worked out fine. On Tuesday morning Russ Kowalchuk's virtue shone with its radiance restored. Earlier, Art Potter, the politically astute president of the Canadian Amateur Hockey Association, had confided to a Canadian reporter, 'These are cold war tactics to demoralize the Canadian team. They always stab us in the back here.' But now even he was satisfied. Witnesses swore there was no girl in the lobby. The Malmen Hotel apologized. Russ Kowalchuk, after all, was a nice clean-living Canadian boy. In the late watches of the night he did not lust after Swedish girls, but possibly, like Bobby Kromm and Don Freer, yearned for nothing more depraved than a ping-pong table. A McIntosh apple maybe.

Finally, the Smoke Eaters did not behave badly in Stockholm. They were misunderstood. They also finished fourth.

Watching Luis Miguel Dominguin fight in Valencia in 1951, I suddenly saw a scrawny boy, two rows down, leap from his seat, vault the *barrera*, broomstick and sack in hand, and make it clear on to the sands of the bull ring, stamping his foot for the bull to charge. Around me people were cheering or laughing warmly, but I remember watching the boy, my heart hammering, until attendants hustled him off. I did not yet know that these boys, called *espontaneos*, were commonplace. A week later, in Paris, a friend showed me a new French communist party publication, a *Life*-size picture magazine lampoon about America. On the first page there was a photograph of Harry Truman, then president, looking bumpkinish as he waved a shoe aloft at an American shoe convention. Opposite, Al Capone smiled darkly behind a cigar, and there was a quote from him endorsing capitalism. The best system, Capone said. On the following page, clinching the case for bestiality, there was a full-page spread of a behemoth of a football player: crouching, the eyes mean, the mouth snarling, arms hanging ape-like. This, the caption said, was a typical American university student.

I toss in these two memories, seemingly unrelated, because at the bullfight in Valencia it did not occur to me that a gifted reporter, mulling over just such a bit of adolescent daring, as George Plimpton once did, could develop it into two unusual sports books: *Out Of My League*, published in 1962, and now *Paper Lion*. And then I have always shared what I take to be the French communist party line on American football. I am, I should hastily add, not so much a fellow traveller as a committed sports fan. Living in England for more than twelve years, I follow the baseball and ice hockey results conscientiously in the Paris *Herald*, but football, even after reading Plimpton's uncommonly good *Paper Lion*, is still alien to me. Possibly my prejudice against football, like just about everything else, breaks down to race and class. On our street, a working-class street, we wanted to be boxers or, failing that, baseball pitchers. Bonus boys. Speaking for myself, I got so far as to train for the Golden Gloves when I unfortunately came up against a schoolmate called Manny, who was already fighting professionally, working in preliminaries under an alias in small towns. Manny had the unnerving habit of blowing his nose on his glove before swatting me. I still insist he didn't knock me out. Revolted, I fainted. In Montreal we had the example of Maxie Berger, who fought in the Garden and once went the distance with Ike Williams; and we also had our one and only Ziggy 'The Fireball' Freed, who would have been a star with the Athletics had Connie Mack not been such a lousy anti-semite. Ziggy was actually signed by a scout at the age of eighteen and was sent out for seasoning with a Class 'D' team in the Carolinas. He lasted only a season. 'You think they'd give a Jewish boy a chance to pitch out there?' he asked. 'Sure, in the ninth inning, with the bases loaded and none out, with their homerun hitter coming up to the plate, the manager would shout, O.K., Ziggy, it's your ball game now.'

Football, however, was always remote. A middle-class WASP's game. I still associate it with hip flasks, racoon coats, and loud boring McGill alumni making damn fools of themselves in downtown Montreal. I also have a problem with the players, the boors of my university days. Of James Thurber's university days too, if you remember Bolenciecwcz, the Ohio State University tackle, in *My Life And Hard Times*. 'In order to be eligible to play,' Thurber wrote, 'it was necessary for him to keep up on his studies, a very difficult matter for while he was no dumber than an ox he was not any smarter.' Bassum, the economics professor, asks the star tackle to name a means of transportation ('Just any means of transportation. That is, any medium, agency, or method of getting from one place to another.'), but this he is unable to do. 'Toot-toot-toot,' the professor says. 'Choo-choo-choo.' Finally, Bolenciecwcz comes up with train, thereby qualifying for the Illinois game.

I've been to pro games, and I can't help feeling that there is something fundamentally unsportsman-like about men, mostly oversize to begin with, strapping themselves into all that outlandish equipment and wearing cages to protect their faces, all for a game's sake. It's brutish. In the epilogue to *Paper Lion*, Plimpton writes, 'Detroit had a bad season my year. The team finished fourth in its division. . . . Injuries hurt their chances. Eleven of the first-line players were knocked out of the line-up with injuries, most of them on the defensive team. Joe Schmidt and Carl Brettschneider of the linebackers were crippled, and so were Yale Lary and Night Train Lane. Gary Lowe ruptured his achilles tendon. . . .'

If I have already made it abundantly clear that football isn't exactly my game, then I must say that George Plimpton's *Paper Lion* is at once a more satisfying and complex book than *Out Of My League*, wherein the writer unwinds the sometimes nightmarish story of how he came to pitch to an all-star line-up of National and American League players in the Yankee Stadium, the team with the most hits picking up a thousand dollars.

Plimpton got *Sports Illustrated* to put up the pot. It was his notion, he told the editor, that he would pitch 'not as a hotshot – that'd be a different story – but as a guy who's average, really, a sort of Mr. Everybody, the sort who thinks he's a fair athlete. . . .' If it worked out, he hoped to go on to play tennis with Pancho Gonzalez, box with Archie Moore, play golf with Snead or Hogan, and so forth.

The writing in *Out Of My League* is fresh and observant, but it suffers from spinning out a one-day adventure into a book. It is original, there is much to admire, but I think it would have read better as a shorter piece, like John Updike's splendid account of Ted Williams' last day with the Boston Red Sox. Ultimately, the most compelling thing about *Out Of My League* is what I can only call the author's *chutzpah*, his actually going through with it, imposing himself on the players and the unsuspecting crowd at the Yankee Stadium. Many of the players were indifferent, others were cold. With Plimpton floundering on the mound, Mantle yawns ostentatiously. But then we never really worry about the author's pitching performance *per se* as we do, say about Jim Brosnan's good and bad days in *The Long Season*. Plimpton's professional pride, unlike Brosnan's, could never be truly involved. Neither is his livelihood.

We also do not fret about how Plimpton will stack up on the field as the Detroit Lions' last-string quarterback, but from the moment he begins haphazard practice, whacking a football into an armchair in his apartment, until he is finally allowed to call five plays in an inter-squad scrimmage at Pontiac, Plimpton holds us with the force of sheer good writing. His account of his stay with the Lions makes for a most enjoyable, likeable book. If he was, predictably, a disaster on the field, I can think of no other non-fiction book that evokes more successfully the special taste and feeling of a game and the men who play it.

To begin with, Plimpton had trouble getting a team to allow him to work out with them, let alone take part in an actual game. Red Hickey, coach of the Western Conference All-Stars, said. 'Did I hear you right? You – with no experience – want to train and then *play* – in the Pro-Bowl game?'

The New York Giants wouldn't have him and neither would the Jets. Fortunately George Wilson, the earthy coach of the Detroit Lions, was amused by the idea and invited Plimpton to camp. From the moment of his arrival, Plimpton reveals a necessarily good and receptive nature and an enviable eye for detail. Of course he's got a lot going for him. Even a runthrough of some of the names on the Detroit roster has a distinctive tang to it: Milton Plum, Yale Lary, Nick Pietrosante, Dick LeBeau, Scooter McLean. . . . as well as a linesman, nicknamed the Mad Creeper, who was, Plimpton writes, a near pathological case.

> 'No one knew who the Mad Creeper was. . . . His habit was to creep along the corridors late at night, three or four in the morning, sneak into someone's room, lean over his bed and throttle him hard and briefly, just closing his hands around the fellow's throat and then skittering off down the corridor, listening to the gasping behind him.'

The trade idiom is rich. Night Train Lane speaks of his 'captainship', tells how you get 'a great communion to get to the Hall of Fame', and teases Plimpton about the unstoppable Roger Brown the night before the inter-squad scrimmage. 'Jawge, you set to find if Roger's going to *disjoin* you? I mean in Pontiac you are goin' to have expectation in this whole question – he's goin' be at you shufflin' and breathin' *hard*.'

Paper Lion is very rewarding on superfans and hangers-on, including a tailor who has become a touchstone to the rookies. Before the rookies know whether or not they've made the squad, the tailor, who has the ear of the coaches, may come to measure them for a team blazer. Conversely, he may pass them by. Plimpton seems to catch exactly the tension between rookie and veteran, the competition for jobs; the night of the team out-offs; and the nerves that build up before a game, even an exhibition game. Originally, Plimpton had hoped to pass for just another rookie, but Wayne Walker, a regular, had read *Out Of My League*. This killed Plimpton's ready-made (and libellous) excuse for his own ineptitude, the bare-faced lie that he had once been good enough to play ball with a semi-pro Canadian team, the Newfoundland Newfs.

Canadian pro football, let me point out at once, gives gainful employment to many an American journeyman player, as long as he is able to adjust to a slight difference in rules, such as the need to say, Excuse me, before tackling. Then, just as we came through for the United States during prohibition, the year Plimpton was maligning us in Detroit, my permissive country was able to take on several first-line NFL players who had been suspended for gambling. Neither is the Canadian game without its glories. Only a few years ago our Super-Bowl, the Grey Cup game, had to be called in the third quarter because of fog. It was no longer necessary to conceal the ball. Players couldn't find each other and fans couldn't see the field. A moment in sports history, I think, which rivals the 1954 boat race, when Cambridge sank.

Before Plimpton left to join the Lions, a friend in New York, who had once played for the Washington Redskins, warned him about the stupidity of ball players and told him to expect juvenile behaviour. The barracks room humour of the camp (water pistols, jock straps) does seem more than a bit overhearty at times, but Plimpton makes a convincing case for similar lapses among supposedly loftier groups, such as *New Yorker* staff writers; and I must admit that I found the fright masks funny. Working off tensions, it seems that some nights the players would don masks made of thin pliable rubber, vampire heads, Frankenstein monsters, and sneak up on a sleeping team mate to startle him.

Curiously, it is not until page 300 of *Paper Lion*, that Plimpton goes into the question of salaries and bonuses, and then only fleetingly, almost as though talk about money embarrasses him. But, as Red Smith has written again and again, there is no question that the name of the game is money, and that these are men being paid to play a boy's game. One needn't be a football fan to know about the 400,000 dollars paid to Joe Namath for signing with the New York Jets, the bigger bonuses that have been handed out to others since, and the 15,000 dollars earned by each of the Green Bay Packers for a day's work against the Kansas City Chiefs. At the risk of sounding old-fashioned, it goes against the grain. This sort of reward *is* socially unbalanced. I would have liked to know more about the money in the game and what the players felt about it. Without asking for a grey, sociological work rather than the lively journal Plimpton has given us, I still could have done with decidedly more information about the economics of the football business and the profits involved.

Sports, obviously, is a bloody big business, a growth industry, as they say, with the National Hockey League expanding to twelve teams next season, new professional basketball and soccer leagues promised, and the purses offered on the PGA circuit the highest ever. If the profits to be made out of sports is immense, just possibly immorally high, then club owners differ from the tycoons in other industries by asking for our hearts as well as our money. We are entreated to trust them with our boyish admiration and enthusiasm, with what we retain of the old school holler, at an age when we are more immediately concerned with falling hair, mortgages, and choosing schools for the kids. Going back through the years, I think the first time I felt socially betrayed, lied to by anyone outside my immediate family, was when I discovered that the Montreal Royals, my home baseball team, was not made up of natives but largely southern crackers. This, of course, was long before club owners had the courage to move their franchises about so cynically. Going wherever the biggest profits were.

Professional sports, though I am still addicted to them, have begun to alienate me in yet another way. It was George Plimpton's notion that as a sort of Mr. Everybody, a Central Park quarter-back, a Sunday pitcher, he would try his hand at baseball, football, and other sports. James Thurber, he told the editor of *Sports Illustrated*, once wrote that the majority of American males put themselves to sleep by striking out the batting order of the New York Yankees. Yes; but if at one time Plimpton's idea of testing himself, seeing how well he could do in pro company, seemed a feasible, even charming conceit, I fear it is considerably less so today. If once athletes were really rather like us, only more beautifully made, better conditioned, more gifted, suddenly too many of them are not like us at all. All at once basketball players tend to be seven foot tall and football players weigh three hundred pounds. Then football, rather more than most sports, has come to suffer from over-specialization, with different teams for offence and defence. In contrast it would seem that soccer players, all of them sixty minute men, must be far more resourceful. They are certainly more elegant and recognizably human to watch, trotting out on to the field in jerseys and shorts, unarmed, so to speak.

Finally, George Plimpton's *Paper Lion* joins a growing body of first-rate writing about sports: one thinks immediately of Norman Mailer on the fights, Updike and Mark Harris – nevertheless I have a reservation. Much as I enjoyed Plimpton's book, I can't help feeling guilty, like having been to a movie on a fine summer's afternoon. An earlier generation of American writers had to test themselves not against Bart Starr and Archie Moore, but the Spanish Civil War and the Moscow trials. In Europe, Isaac Babel, looking for a change, rode with the Red Cavalry. George Orwell went to Wigan Pier and then Catalonia. Koestler came out of Spain with his *Spanish Testament*. This is not meant to be an attack on Plimpton, but all of us, Plimpton's generation and mine. One day, I fear, we will be put down as a trivial, peripheral bunch. Crazy about bad old movies, nostalgic for comic books. Our gods don't fail. At worst, they grow infirm. They suffer pinched nerves, like Paul Hornung. Or arthritic arms, like Sandy Koufax.

I. ENCYCLOPEDIA OF JEWS IN SPORTS

Good news. The bar mitzvah gift book has come of age. In my time, we had to make do with Paul de Kruif's inspirational medical books or a year's subscription to the National Geographic magazine. Since then, but too late for me, a spill of treasuries has become available: of Jewish Thought, of Jewish Wisdom, of Jewish Humour. Now, after many years of research, filling 'a glaring void in the long record of Jewish achievement', comes the *Encyclopedia of Jews in Sports* by Bernard Postal, Jesse Silver and Roy Silver (Bloch, 526 pp., $12.95), 'the first all-inclusive volume to tell the complete story of Jews in professional and amateur sports all over the world, from Biblical times to Sandy Koufax's no-hitter in September'.

The compendium comes lavishly recommended. 'It is', Mel Allen writes on the jacket flap, 'a noteworthy contribution to mankind's ever-growing quest for knowledge'; while Senator Abraham Ribicoff, former Secretary of Health, Education and Welfare, writes in a foreword, 'Interest in sports among Jews – as among all Americans – has intensified as opportunities for leisure activities have increased.' Continuing in the same thoughtful, controversial vein, he adds, 'For sports are a healthy part of American life, and Jews are involving themselves fully in all aspects of American life.'

The encyclopedia should first of all be judged by its own exacting standards. If I am not guilty of misunderstanding editors Postal, Silver and Silver, they compiled it not to turn a buck in the non-book trade, but for two altogether admirable reasons: that Jews might be made more aware of their sports heritage and to dispel 'one of the oldest myths about the Jew . . . the curious belief that he was a physical coward and a stranger to athletics', or, as Senator Ribicoff puts it, that he is 'nimble in the head, perhaps, but not too nimble with the feet'. On this test alone, the encyclopedia fails. It will, I fear, make trouble for *us* with *them*. It's dynamite! Rotten with proof of Jewish duplicity and athletic ineptitude.

Until I read the encyclopedia, for instance, I had no idea that Mushy Callaghan (World Junior Welterweight Champion, 1926–30) was really born Vincente Morris Schneer, and I wonder if this will also be a revelation to his Irish Catholic fans. Neither did I suspect that anybody called Al McCoy (World Middleweight Champion, 1914–17) answered more properly to the name Al Rudolph, and was actually the son of a kosher butcher who had changed his name because his parents objected to his boxing activities.

Then consider these far from untypical baseball entries:

'COHEN, HYMAN "HY." Pitcher, b. Jan. 29, 1931 in Brooklyn, N.Y. Played for Chicago Cubs in 1955. Total Games: 7. Pitching record: 0–0. Right-hander.'

'HERTZ, STEVE ALLAN. Infielder, b. Feb. 26, 1945 in Dayton, Ohio. Played for Houston in 1964. Total Games: 5. Batting Average: 000.'

Is this the stuff the Jewish Hall of Fame is made of? Doesn't it suggest that in order to fill only 526 pages with Jewish athletic 'Achievement' Messrs. Postal, Silver and Silver were driven to scraping the bottom of the barrel, so to speak? Still worse. Put this volume in the hands of an anti-Semitic sportsman and can't you just hear him say. 'Nimble in the feet? Ho ho! Among them 0–0 pitchers and nothing hitters count as *athletes*.'

Orthodox Jews will also be distressed by certain entries in the encyclopedia. Was it necessary, for example, to include Cardinal, Conrad Ceth, a pitcher with an 0–1 record when he is only half Jewish? Or the playboy pitcher Belinsky, Robert

'Bo', just because he is the son of a Jewish mother? This is more than a purist's racial quibble. Such entries could lead, if this volume is the first of a series, to the inclusion of, say, Elizabeth Taylor in a compilation of Jewish Playmates from Biblical Times to Today.

Of course there is another possibility. Half-Jewish players of dubious achievement were included in the book because the editors are not only racialists, but cunning ones at that, and what they intended by listing Belinsky and Cardinal was an oblique but penetrating comment on the capabilities of the issue of mixed marriages.

Something else. You and I might be pleased in our hearts to know that the first man to take money for playing baseball, the first real pro, was a Jew, Lipman E. 'Lip' Pike, whose name appeared in a box score for the first time only one week after his bar mitzvah in 1864, but anti-Semites could easily make something unfortunate out of this information. Neither was I proud to discover that, according to a Talmudic scholar at the Jewish Theological Seminary of America, Jews – as early as the second century, C.E. – had a special prayer for horse players; and that the bettor was advised to 'take this (prayer) tablet and bury it in the ground of the hippodrome where you want to win'.

There are some regrettable omissions. While Joe Reichler earns an entry because he is a baseball writer and Allen Roth, resident statistician with the Montreal Canadiens, is also included, there is no mention anywhere of Mailer, Norman, who has reported memorably on boxing for *Esquire*. Neither could I find the names of Malamud, Bernard, author of a baseball novel, or Schulberg, Budd, who has written a novel about boxing. Does this suggest an anti-intellectual bias on the part of Messrs. Postal, Silver and Silver?

This is not to say that the *Encyclopedia of Jews in Sports* is entirely without merit. The three-page ice hockey section pleased me enormously if only because it included my favourite Jewish defenseman, one-time National League player, the astute Larry Zeidal. An issue of *Jewish Press*, a New York publication, once carried the following Canadian report: 'ONLY JEW IN PRO HOCKEY PLAYS A ROUGH GAME.' 'Larry Zeidal', the story began, 'owns a scar for every one of the 20 years he marauded through organized hockey. "When you're the only Jew in this bloody game," he said, "you have to prove you can take the rough stuff more than the average player." ' The story went on to say that Zeidal, in contrast to his team-mates, read *Barron's Business Weekly* between periods, perhaps taking 'Lip' Pike as his inspiration. Pike, the encyclopedia notes, played baseball at a time when other players were usually gamblers and drunkards. 'However, Pike was an exception. Throughout his career contemporary journals commented on his sobriety, intelligence, wit, and industry.'

Finally, if the encyclopedia fails, on balance, to rectify the oldest myth about the Jew – that he is 'a stranger to athletics' – it must be allowed that this is a pioneering work and a step in the right direction. Let us hope that Messrs. Postal, Silver and Silver, thus encouraged, will now take on other foul anti-Semitic myths, for instance, that Jews don't drink or practise homosexuality widely enough. I, for one, look forward to an encyclopedia (for delinquent bar mitzvah boys, perhaps) on Jewish Drunks, High School Dropouts, and Thugs from Noah to today. I would also like to see a compilation of Famous Jewish Homosexuals, Professional and Amateur, Throughout History.

II. KOUFAX THE INCOMPARABLE

Within many a once-promising, now suddenly command-generation Jewish writer, there is a major league ball player waiting to leap out; and come Sunday mornings in summer, from the playing fields of East Hampton to the Bois de

Boulogne to Hyde Park, you can see them, heedless of tender discs and protruding bellies, out in the fresh air together, playing ball. We were all raised on baseball. While today there do not seem to be that many Jewish major league stars about, when I was a kid there were plenty we could identify with: Sid Gordon and Al Rosen and of course Hank Greenberg. Even in Montreal we had, for a time, one of our own in the outfield, Kermit Kitman. Kitman, alas, was all field and no hit and never graduated from the Royals to the parent Dodgers, but it was once our schoolboy delight to lie in wait for him over the clubhouse at Saturday afternoon games and shout, 'Hey, Kermit, you *pipick*-head, you think it's right for you to strike out on *Shabbes*?'

Baseball was never a bowl of cherries for the Jewish player. *The Encyclopedia of Jews in Sports* observes that while the initial ballplayer to accept money for playing was a Jew, Lipman E. Pike, there were few known Jewish players. The *Sporting News*, in 1902, wrote of one player, 'His name was Cohen and he assumed the name of Kane when he became a semi-professional, because he fancied that there was a popular and professional prejudice against Hebrews as ball players.' Other major-leaguers were more militantly Jewish. Barney Pelty, for instance, who pitched for the St. Louis Browns from 1903 to 1912, seemingly did not object to being known as 'The Yiddish Curver'. Still, the number of our players in any era has been small, possibly because, as Norm Sherry, once a catcher with the Dodgers, has said, 'Many boys find opposition at home when they want to go out for a ball-playing career.' Despite opposition at home or in the game, the Jew, as the *Encyclopedia* happily notes, has won virtually every honour in baseball. If there remains a Jewish Problem in the game today, it hinges on the Rosh Hashanah-Yom Kippur syndrome, for the truth we all have to live with is that much as the Reform temple has done to lighten our traditional Jewish burdens, the rush for the pennant and

Rosh Hashanah, the World Series and Yom Kippur, still sometimes conflict.

Should a nice Jewish boy play ball on the High Holidays? Historical evidence is inconclusive. Harry Eisenstadt, once a pitcher for the Dodgers, was in uniform but not scheduled to pitch on Rosh Hashanah, 1935, but when the Giants began to hurt his team he was called into the game and his first pitch was hit for a grand slam home-run. And yet – and yet – one year earlier, Hank Greenberg, with the Tigers close to their first pennant since 1909, played on Rosh Hashanah and hit two home-runs. Greenberg went to *shul* on Yom Kippur, alas, and the Tigers lost. The whole country, rabbis and fans at odds, was involved in the controversy, and Edgar Guest was sufficiently inspired to write a poem the last verse of which reads:

> Come Yom Kippur – holy fast day
> world-wide over to the Jew –
> And Hank Greenberg to his teaching
> and the old tradition true
> Spent the day among his people
> and
> he didn't come to play.
> Said Murphy to Mulrooney 'We
> shall lose the game today!
> We shall miss him in the infield
> and
> shall miss him at the bat,
> But he's true to his religion –
> and
> I honour him for that!'

Honour him, yes, but it is possible that Greenberg, the only Jew in the Hall of Fame, was also tragically inhibited by his Jewish heritage. I'm thinking of 1938, when he had hit 58 home runs, two short of Babe Ruth's record, but with five games to play, failed to hit another one out of the park. Failed . . . or just possibly held back, because Greenberg just possibly understood that if he shattered the Babe's record, seemingly inviolate, it would be considered pushy of him and given the climate of the times, not be such a good thing for the Jews.

Greenberg, in any event, paved the way for today's outstanding Jewish player, the incomparable Sandy Koufax. So sensitive is the Dodger front office to Koufax's religious feelings that Walter Alston, the Dodgers' manager, who was once severely criticized for scheduling him to play on Yom Kippur, is now reported to keep a Jewish calendar on his desk.

Koufax, who has just published his autobiography, is not only the best Jewish hurler in history, he may well be the greatest pitcher of all time, regardless of race, colour or creed. His fast ball, Bob Feller has said, 'is just as good as mine', and Casey Stengel was once moved to comment, 'If that young fella was running for office in Israel, they'd have a whole new government over there. . . .' Koufax has won the National League's Most Valuable Player Award, the Cy Young Award as the outstanding major league pitcher of the year, and the Hickok Pro Athlete of the Year Award. He has pitched four no-hit games, more than any other major league pitcher. He holds the major league record for both the most shutouts and the most strikeouts in one season and also the major league record for the number of seasons in which he has struck out more than three hundred batters. He has tied the major league record for most strikeouts in a nine-inning game, and also tied World Series records. I could go on and on, but a nagging question persists. This, you'd think, was enough, Koufax, at least, has proved himself. He is accepted. But is he?

Anti-Semitism takes many subtle shapes and the deprecating story one reads again and again, most memorably recorded in *Time*, is that Sandy Koufax is actually something of an intellectual. He doesn't mix. Though he is the highest-paid player in the history of the game, improving enormously on Lipman E. Pike's $20 a week, he considers himself above it. Fresco Thompson, a Dodger vice-president, is quoted as saying, 'What kind of a line is he drawing anyway – between himself and the world, between himself and the team?' Another report quotes Koufax himself as saying, 'The last thing that entered my mind was becoming a professional athlete. Some kids dream of being a ball player, I wanted to be an architect. In fact, I didn't like baseball. I didn't think I'd ever like it.' And the infamous *Time* story relates that when Koufax was asked how he felt after winning the last game in the 1965 World Series, he said, 'I'm just glad it's over and I don't have to do this again for four whole months.'

In *Koufax*, which the pitcher wrote with the dubious relief help of one Ed Linn, he denies the accuracy of most of these stories. In fact, looked at one way, Koufax's autobiography can be seen as a sad effort at self-vindication, a forced attempt to prove once and for all that he is the same as anybody else. Possibly, Koufax protests too much. 'I have nothing against myths,' he begins, 'but there is one myth that has been building through the years that I would just as soon bury without any particular honors: the myth of Sandy Koufax, the anti-athlete.' He goes on to state flatly that he is no 'dreamy intellectual' lured out of college by a big bonus, which he has since regretted, and as if to underline this point, he immediately lapses into regular-guy English. 'Look, if I could act that good I'd have signed with 20th Century Fox instead of Brooklyn. . . .' Koufax protests that though he is supposed to read Aldous Huxley and Thomas Wolfe, and listen to Beethoven, Bach and Mendelssohn, if anybody dropped in at his place they would more likely find him listening to a show tune or a Sinatra album. All the same, he does own up to a hi-fi. 'I wish', he writes, 'my reading tastes were classier, but they happen to run to the bestseller list and the book-club selections', which strikes this reader as something of an evasion. Which book clubs, Sandy? Literary Guild or Readers' Subscription?

Koufax insists the only thing he was good at in school was athletics (He captained the basketball team which won the National Jewish Welfare Board hoop tournament in 1951–52) and denies, to quote *Time* again, that he is an anti-athlete 'who suffers so little from pride that he does not even possess a photograph of himself' .If you walk into his room, Koufax writes, 'you are overwhelmed by a huge, immodest action painting', by which he means a picture which shows him in four successive positions of delivery. Furthermore, he denies that 'I'm mightily concerned about projecting a sparkling All-American image', and yet it seems to me this book has no other purpose. Examined on any other level it is a very bush-league performance, thin cliché-ridden, and slapped together with obnoxiously clever chapter headings such as, 'Where the Games Were', '*La Dolce Vita* of Vero Beach', 'Suddenly That Summer', and 'California, Here We – Oops – Come'. A chapter called 'The Year of The Finger', I should hasten to add in this time of Girodias and Grove Press books, actually deals with Koufax's near tragic circulatory troubles, his suspected case of Reynaud's Phenomenon.

Projecting an All-American image or not, Koufax hasn't one unkind or, come to think of it, perceptive word to say about the game or any of his team-mates. Anecdotes with a built-in twinkle about this player or that unfailingly end with 'That's John (Roseboro)', or 'That's Lou (Johnson)', and one of his weightiest observations runs 'Life is odd', which, *pace* Fresco Thompson, is not enough to imply alienation.

Still true to the All-American image, Koufax writes, nicely understating the case, that though there are few automobiles he couldn't afford today, nothing has given him more joy than the maroon Rollfast bicycle his grandparents gave him for his tenth birthday when he was just another Rockville Centre kid. 'An automobile is only a means of transportation. A bike to a ten-year-old boy is a magic carpet and a status symbol and a gift of love.' Self-conscious, perhaps, about his towering salary, which he clearly deserves, considering what a draw he is at the gate, he claims that most of the players were for him and Drysdale during their 1966 holdout. 'The players felt – I hope – that the more we got paid, the more they would get paid in the future', which may be stretching a point some.

Koufax was not an instant success in baseball. He was, to begin with, an inordinately wild pitcher, and the record for his 1955 rookie year was 2–2. The following year he won two more games, but lost four, and even in 1960 his record was only 8–13. Koufax didn't arrive until 1961, with an 18–13 record, and though some accounts tell of his dissatisfaction with the earlier years and even report a bitter run-in with Dodgers' general manager, Buzzy Bavasi – because Koufax felt he was not getting sufficient work – he understandably soft-pedals the story in his autobiography. Koufax is also soft on Alston, who, according to other sources, doubted that the pitcher would ever make it.

If Koufax came into his own in 1961 – becoming a pitcher, he writes, as distinct from a thrower – then his transmogrification goes some way to belie the All-American image; in fact there is something in the story that will undoubtedly appeal to anti-Semites who favour the Jewish-conspiracy theory of history. Koufax, according to his own account, was helped most by two other Jews on the team, Allen Roth, the resident statistician, and Norm Sherry, a catcher. The turning-point, Koufax writes, came during spring training, at an exhibition game, when Sherry told him, 'Don't try to throw hard, because when you force your fast ball you're always high with it. Just this once, try it my way. . . .'

'I had heard it all before,' Koufax writes. 'Only, for once, it wasn't blahblahblah. For once I was rather convinced. . . .' Koufax pitched Sherry's way and ended up with a seven-inning no-hitter and went on from there to super-stardom. The unasked question is, would Norm Sherry have done as much for Don Drysdale?

III. POSTSCRIPT

Koufax The Incomparable appeared in *Commentary*, November, 1966, and led to a heated correspondence:

MARSHALL ADESMAN, BROOKLYN, N.Y., WROTE:

As a professional athlete in the highest sense of the word, Hank Greenberg would never have purposely failed to tie or break Ruth's record. The material gain he could have realized by attaining this goal would have been matched only by the great prestige and glory that naturally come along with the magical figure of sixty home-runs. Greenberg failed only because the pressure, magnified tenfold by the press, weighed too heavily on his shoulders. Very rarely is one able to hit the ball into the seats when he is seeking to do so. Home-runs come from natural strokes of the bat, and Greenberg's stroke in those last five games was anything but natural. The pitchers, also, were not giving the Detroit slugger anything too good to hit, not wishing to have the dubious honor of surrendering number sixty. In short, it was the pressure that made Greenberg's bat too heavy, not the political atmosphere. Perhaps Mr. Richler should check his facts before his next article on the National Pastime.

SAMUEL HEFT, LONG BEACH, N.Y., WROTE:

I am stunned by . . . some startling statements made by Mordecai Richler. . . .

Even to hint at the possibility that the Hall of Fame baseball player, Hank Greenberg, 'held back' in his efforts to break Babe Ruth's home run record, for any reason, is shocking. To state that Greenberg considered it would be 'pushy' of him to do so, is almost too silly for comment. I shudder to think of a player in the Hall of Fame being accused of not giving his all. . . .

Richler states that 'many boys found opposition at home' when they went out for sports. This is understandable. Our parents were not sports-minded, because of their European sufferings. . . . I'm sure our people didn't get many opportunities to play ball in the *shtetl*, while running away from pogroms.

I disagree that there is a Jewish problem in baseball today. If Walter Alston keeps a Jewish calendar on his desk . . . it is because he is a good administrator, and needs this reminder in his scheduling of pitchers' rotations, and not because of 'sensitivity.'

So far as playing baseball on the Jewish holidays goes, and yelling *pipickhead* at Kermit, this is not a baseball problem. I see with my own eyes too many Jews of all denominations mowing lawns, shopping, and doing numerous other chores on the *Shabbes*. . . .

Mr. Richler's article may do serious harm in the struggle against discrimination. . . . Maybe, according to Richler, even Kermit Kitman might have been a good hitter, but he was afraid the Montreal non-Jewish population would think he was 'pushy.'

E. KINTISCH, ALEXANDRIA, VIRGINIA, WROTE:

. . . Richler very obviously doesn't think much of Koufax. Then why did he bother reading the Koufax book, or writing about it? . . .

I am but one of approximately two-to-three dozen Jewish
baseball writers – writers from big city newspapers – who
cover major league baseball teams from the beginning of
spring training through the World Series – and as such
should inform your readers that Mordecai Richler was off
base quite a few times in his 'Koufax the Incomparable.'
(November 1966)

Richler indicates that Hank Greenberg was 'tragically
inhibited by his Jewish heritage' and thus held back and hit
58 home runs instead of breaking Babe Ruth's record of 60
because the breaking of such a record '. . . would be considered pushy of him . . . and not a good thing for the Jews.'
Balderdash! Greenberg didn't hit 60 because pitchers stopped
giving him anything good to hit at – probably because he
was Jewish, and probably also because no pitcher wants to
be remembered for throwing historic home run balls. We
must assume also that the pressure was a factor, as it always
is; what also hurt was that a season-ending doubleheader
(in Cleveland) had to be moved to a bigger ball park with a
longer left field, and that the second game wasn't played to a
nine-inning finish. . . .

I agree that the *Time* magazine cover story on Koufax was
distorted, but to accuse *Time* of anti-Semitism is presumptuous. *Time* has erred on plenty of other sports cover stories
as have many of the other slicks. The image of Koufax as an
intellectual (which he is not) was featured, I suspect, because
it made 'a good angle' and probably because a *Time* stringer
spotted a bookshelf. Moreover, that Koufax likes his privacy
isn't unusual. Many star players, Feller, Musial, Williams *et al.*,
roomed alone in their later years and did their best to avoid
the mob.

Author Richler is looking too hard, also, when he emphasizes that Koufax, in his autobiography, points out that he was helped most by two other Jews ... Sherry, a catcher, advised Koufax not to throw hard, advice I'm sure Sherry has given to dozens and dozens of Gentile pitchers, and advice which previously had been given to Koufax by Gentile coaches. Sherry simply happened to mention this at precisely the right moment, before a meaningless exhibition game, and when Koufax was ... eager to listen. ...

As for Allen Roth, he was a statistician with the Dodgers, the only full-time statistician employed by a big league club. Roth borders on genius in this field. It was his job to keep and translate his findings to the Dodger players and the Dodger management. Whatever information Roth gave Koufax (and I don't know what this was), I'm sure was part of the routine. Richler's attitude is disgusting if he thinks that Roth would favour Koufax because both are Jews. In effect, Richler is saying that Roth would withhold significant statistics from Gentiles such as Drysdale, Newcombe, or Podres.

I agree that from a so-called Jewish standpoint, the Koufax book is disappointing, and I agree with Richler that Koufax protesteth too much in emphasizing that he is not anti-athlete. It is unfortunate that Koufax didn't control his anger, not only at the *Time* story but at several minor pieces that preceded it. In his book, Koufax tells us almost nothing about his Jewishness; that he is Jewish is mentioned almost in passing. But he doesn't owe us any detailed explanations. As a baseball book, and as a text in pitching, I found it excellent.

I should think that *Commentary*, in this rare instance when it did touch on sports, could have done better than offer the long-distance musings of a novelist. ...

AMRAM M. DUCOVNY, NEW YORK CITY, WRITES:

I am shocked that Mr. Richler in his treatise on Curve Balls: Are They Good or Bad for the Jews? overlooked Willie

Davis's three errors in one innings behind Koufax in the 1966 World Series – which was one of the most flagrant acts of Negro anti-Semitism since the Panic of 1908.

He does get somewhere in pointing out the Jewish-conspiracy angle in the Norm Sherry-Koufax cabal; however, he does not really go deep enough. What of Norm's brother Larry – also a Dodger pitcher at the time – stopped from the advice that made a super start because of piddling sibling rivalry? There's one for Bill Stern!

And yea, verily, let us weep for the likes of Don Drysdale – disenfranchised WASP – alone in a sea of Gentile coaches whose knowledge of baseball never had the benefit of the secret indoctrination into the *Protocols of the Elders of Swat*. By the way, what is that resident genius, Norm Sherry, doing today? Have I somehow missed his name among the current great pitching coaches of baseball?

And finally, finally, the true story of the whispered Greenberg caper, wherein he was visited by representatives of the Anti-Defamation League, the American Jewish Committee and Congress, and the many, many Friends of the Hebrew University, who said unto him: 'Hershel, thou shalt not Swat; whither Ruth goest, thou goest not.'

I am looking forward with great anticipation to Mr. Richler's exposure of Mike Epstein (the self-labeled 'super-Jew' rookie of the Baltimore Orioles) who all 'insiders' know is a robot created at a secret plant in the Negev and shipped to Baltimore for obvious chauvinistic reasons.

FINALLY THAT VERY GOOD WRITER, DAN WAKEFIELD, WROTE A MOST AMUSING LETTER THAT BEGAN:

I greatly enjoyed Mordecai Richler's significant comments on Sandy Koufax, and the profound questions he raised about the role of Jews in American sports. Certainly much research still needs to be done in this area, and I hope that some of the

provocative points raised by Richler will be picked up and
followed through by our social scientists, many of whom are
capable of turning, say, a called strike into a three-volume
study of discrimination in the subculture of American
athletics.

I REPLIED:

The crucial question is: did Hank Greenberg hold back
(possibly for our sake), or was the pressure too much for him?
Mr. Adesman, obviously a worldly man, suggests that Greenberg couldn't have held back, because of 'the material gain
he could have realized' by hitting sixty home-runs. This, it
seems to me, is gratuitously attributing coarse motives to an
outstanding Jewish sportsman.

Mr. Heft is stunned by my flattering notion that Greenberg
might have placed the greater Jewish good above mere
athletic records and goes on to nibble at a theory of Jewish
anti-gamesmanship based on our parents' 'running away
from pogroms.' This theory, clearly unattractive if developed
to its logical big league conclusion, would surely have
resulted in a more noteworthy Jewish record on the base
paths. Mr. Heft is also of the opinion that if Walter Alston
keeps a Jewish calendar on his desk, it is because he is a good
administrator. Yom Kippur, Mr. Heft, comes but once a
year, and surely Alston doesn't require a calendar to remind
him of one date. If Koufax had also been unwilling to take
his turn on the mound on Tisha be'Av or required, say, a
chometz-free resin bag for the Passover week, then Alston
would have had a case. As things stand, the calendar must be
reckoned ostentatious.

About Kermit Kitman: I'm afraid his poor hitting had no
racial origins, but was a failure all his own, regardless of race,
colour, or creed. His superb fielding, however, was another
matter: a clear case of the overcompensating Jew. Briefly put,
Kitman was a notorious *chapper*, a grabber, that is to say any

74

fly ball hit into the outfield had to be *his* fly ball, if you know what I mean.

Mr. Kintisch errs. I admire Koufax enormously and shall miss him sorely this season. He was undoubtedly the greatest pitcher of our time, and yet – and yet – now that he has retired so young is it possible that carping anti-Semites have already begun the whispering campaign: great, yes, but *sickly*. Without the staying power of Warren Spahn. An unnatural athlete.

Jerome Holtzman, a dazzling intellectual asset to the sports department of the Chicago *Sun-Times*, raises darker questions. Greenberg, he says, would never have held back. He 'didn't hit 60 because pitchers stopped giving him anything good to hit at – *probably because he was Jewish. . . .*' Now there's something nasty even I didn't think of: the possibility that Bob Feller, Red Ruffing and others threw bigoted anti-Semitic curve balls at Hank Greenberg whilst a later generation of American League pitchers fed Roger Maris pro-Gentile pitches. . . . Next season I would implore Holtzman and other Jewish baseball writers to keep a sharp eye on the racial nature of pitches thrown to (or God forbid, even at) Mike Epstein.

As for *Time*, if it is not anti-Semitic then it is certainly Machiavellian; otherwise, why second-best Juan Marichal on a cover last summer when Koufax was also available? Either as a back-of-the-hand to Jewish achievement or as a shameful, possibly Jewish-motivated, attempt to apply the famous *Time* cover jinx to the one Gentile who might have won more games than Koufax.

Messrs. Ducovny and Wakefield are another matter. They think I would joke about Jews in sport, which strikes me as presumptuous.

Mr. Ducovny cunningly introduces Willie Davis's three errors behind Koufax in one inning and immediately claims this was a case of Negro anti-Semitism. Not necessarily. It depends on whether Davis dropped the three fly balls in his character as a Negro or in his office as an outfielder. Me, I'm keeping an open mind on the incident.

On the other hand, Mr. Wakefield is right when he says there is much more research to be done about Jews in sport. Not only Jews, but other minority and out-groups. Allen Roth, *pace* Jerome Holtzman, may border on genius in his field, but though it may seem to some fans that baseball is already stifled with statistics, these are only statistics of a certain kind, safe statistics. It has been left to me to establish, haphazardly I admit, the absorbing statistic that homosexuals in both major leagues prefer playing third base over all other positions. As a group, they hit better in night games and are more adroit at trapping line drives than catching flies. They do not, as the prejudiced would have it, tend to be showboats. They are a group with a gripe. A valid gripe. Treated as equals on the field, cheered on by teammates when they hit a homer, they tend to be shunned in the showers. On road trips, they have trouble finding roomies.

Finally, since I wrote my article, so unexpectedly controversial, world events have overtaken journalism.

1. Sandy Koufax has retired.
2. Ronald Reagan has been elected governor of California.
3. Tommy Davis has been traded to the Mets.
4. Maury Wills has been given, it would seem, to Pittsburgh.

I'm not saying that Ronald Reagan, who in the unhappy past has been obliged to play second-best man again and again for Jewish producers, has been harbouring resentments ... or is behind the incomparable Koufax's departure from California. I'm not saying that image-conscious Governor Reagan, mindful of right-wing support, was against being photographed shaking hands with Captain Maury Wills on opening day. I'm also not saying that after Willie Davis dropped the three flies, Mr. O'Malley turned to one of his minions and said, 'Davis belongs with the Mets.' Furthermore, I'm not saying that the aforementioned front-office minion could not tell one Davis from another. . . . Just remember as they said in the sports pages of my boyhood, that you read it here first.

'QUIET! A REVOLUTION IS BREWING', begins a recent advertisement for the *New Book of Knowledge*. 'This is Gary. Age 11. He's a new breed of student. A result of the "quiet revolution" in our schools. He's spent happy hours on his project. Away from TV. Away from horror comics. Completely absorbed. Learning! Reading about cocoons, larvae, butterflies. . . .'

No, no, Gary is no new breed. I recognize him. In my day he always did his homework immediately he came home from school. He never ate with his elbows on the table. Or peeked at his sister in the bath. Or shoplifted. Or sent unwanted pianos, ambulances, firemen, and bust developers to the class teacher, the unspeakable Miss Ornstein, who made us suffer creative games, like Information Please or Increasing Your Word Power with the *Reader's Digest*. Gary ate his spinach. He was made president of the Junior Red Cross Club and pinned The Ten Rules of Hygiene over his sink. He didn't sweat, he perspired. And he certainly never swiped a hard earned dime from his father's trousers, the price of a brand-new comic book. Oh, the smell of those new comic books! The sheer, the glossy feel! *Tip-Top, Action, Detective*, and *Famous Funnies*.

Each generation its own nostalgia, its own endearing fantasy-figures. For my generation, born into the depression, beginning to encourage and count pubic hairs during World War II, there was nothing quite like the comic books. While bigger, more mature men were cunningly turning road signs to point in the wrong direction in Sussex, standing firm at Tobruk, Sending For More Japs, holding out at Stalingrad, making atomic bombs, burning Jews and gassing Gypsies; while General ('Old Blood and Guts') Patton was opening the Anglo-American service club in London, saying, 'The idea of these clubs could not be better because undoubtedly it is the destiny of the English and American people to rule the world. . . .' and Admiral William F. ('Bull') Halsey was saying off-the-record, 'I hate Japs. I'm telling you men that if I met a pregnant Japanese woman, I'd kick her in the belly.'; we, the young, the hope of the world, were being corrupted by the violence in comic books. Ask Dr. Frederic Wertham, who wrote in *Seduction Of the Innocent.*

> '. . . . a ten-year-old girl . . . asked me why I thought it was harmful to read Wonder Woman. . . . She saw in her home many good books and I took that as a starting point, explaining to her what good stories and novels were. "Supposing," I told her, "you get used to eating sandwiches made with very strong seasonings, with onions and peppers and highly spiced mustard. You will lose your taste for simple bread and butter and for finer food. The same is true for reading strong comic books. If later you want to read a good novel it may describe how a young boy and girl sit together and watch the rain falling. They talk about themselves and the pages of the book describe what their innermost little thoughts are. This is what is called literature. But you will never be able to appreciate that if in comic book fashion you expect that any minute someone will appear and pitch both of them out of the window." '

Or Kingsley Martin, who wrote that Superman was blond and saw in him the nefarious prototype of the Aryan Nazi. Never mind that Superman, the inspired creation of two Jewish boys, Jerome Siegal and Joe Shuster, was neither blond nor Aryan. It was a good theory. We were also being warped by Captain Marvel. The Human Torch, The Flash, Sheena, Queen of the Jungle, Hawkman, Plastic Man, Sub Mariner, and the Batman and Robin. Our champions; our revenge figures against what seemed a gratuitously cruel adult world.

This is not to say our street was without intellectual dissent. After all social realism was the thing, then.

'There's Tarzan in the jungle, week in and week out,' Solly said, 'and he never once has to shit. It's not true to life.'

'What about Wonder Woman?'

'Wonder Woman's a dame, you schmock.'

Wonder Woman was also a waste of time. Uncouth. Like ketchup in chicken soup. Or lighting up cigarette butts retrieved from the gutter. Reading was for improving the mind, my Aunt Ida said, and to that end she recommended *King's Row* or anything by John Gunther. Wonder Woman, according to Dr. Wertham, was a dyke as well. For boys, a frightening image. For girls, a morbid ideal. Yes, Yes, but as Jules Feiffer observes in his nostalgic *The Great Comic Book Heroes*, 'Whether Wonder Woman was a lesbian's dream I do not know, but I know for a fact she was every Jewish boy's unfantasied picture of the world as it really was. You mean men weren't wicked and weak? . . . You mean women didn't have to be *stronger* than men to survive in the world? Not in *my* house!'

The Batman and Robin, the unsparing Dr. Wertham wrote, were also kinky. 'Sometimes Batman ends up in bed injured and young Robin is shown sitting next to him. At home they lead an idyllic life. They are Bruce Wayne and "Dick" Grayson. Bruce Wayne is described as a "socialite" and the official relationship is that Dick is Bruce's ward. They live in sumptuous quarters with beautiful flowers in large vases. . . . Batman is sometimes shown in a dressing gown. . . . It is like a wish dream of two homosexuals living together.'

Unfortunately I cannot personally vouch for the sexual proclivities of "socialites", but I don't see anything necessarily homosexual in 'beautiful flowers in large vases'. This strikes me as witch-hunting. Sexual McCarthyism. Unless the aforesaid flowers were pansies, which would, I admit, just about clinch the good doctor's case. As, however, he does not specify pansies, we may reasonably assume they were another variety of flora. If so, what? Satyric rambling roses? Jewy yellow daffodils? Droopy impotent peonies? Communist-front orchids? More evidence, please.

Of more significance, perhaps, what Dr. Wertham fails to grasp is that we were already happily clued in on the sex life of our comic book heroes. As far back as 1939, publishers (less fastidious than the redoubtable Captain Maxwell) were offering, at fifty cents each, crude black and white comics which improvised pornographically on the nocturnal, even orgiastic, adventures of our champions. I speak here of GASOLINE ALLEY GANG BANG, DICK TRACY'S NIGHT OUT, BLIND DATE WITH THE DRAGON LADY, and the shocking but liberating CAPTAIN AMERICA MEETS WONDER WOMAN, all of which have long since become collector's items. It is worth pointing out, however, that I never came across anything juicy about Superman and Lois Lane, not even gossip, until dirty-minded intellectuals and Nazis had their say.

Item: Richard Kluger writes (*Partisan Review*, Winter 1966): 'He could, of course, ravage any woman on earth (not excluding Wonder Woman, I daresay). . . . Beyond this, there is a tantalising if somewhat clinical and highly speculative theory about why Superman never bedded down with Lois, never really let himself get hotted up over her; Superman, remember, was the Man of Steel. Consider the consequences of supercoitus and the pursuit of The Perfect Orgasm at the highest level. So Supe, a nice guy, had to sublimate. . . .'

Item: When Whiteman, one of the many Superman derivatives, this one published by the American Nazi Party, is asked whatever became of the original Superman, he replied: 'Old Supey succumbed to the influence of Jew pornography. . . . It seems Superman was putting his X-ray vision to immoral use and was picked up by the vice squad as a Peeping Tom.'

Superman of course was the original superhero. 'Just before the doomed planet Krypton exploded to fragments, a scientist placed his infant son within an experimental rocket-ship, launching it toward earth!' Here Superman was dis-covered and finally adopted by the Kents, who gave him the name Clark. When they died 'it strengthened a determina-tion that had been growing in his mind. Clark decided he must turn his titanic strength into channels that would benefit mankind. And so was created . . . SUPERMAN, champion of the oppressed, the physical marvel, who had sworn to devote his existence to helping those in need.' Because Superman was invincible, he soon became something of a bore. . . . until Mort Weisinger, a National Periodical Pub-lications vice-president who has edited the strip since 1941, thought up an Achilles' heel for him. When exposed to fragments from the planet Krypton, Superman is shorn of his powers and reduced to mere earthly capabilities. A smooth touch, but the fact is the real Superman controversy has always centred on his assumed identity of Clark Kent, a decidedly faint-hearted reporter. Kent adores Lois Lane, who has no time for him. Lois is nutty for Superman, who in true aw shucks tradition has no time for any woman. 'The truth may be', Jules Feiffer writes, 'that Kent existed not for purposes of the story but the reader. He is Superman's opinion of the rest of us, a pointed caricature of what we, the non-criminal element, were really like. His fake identity is our real one.' Well, yes, but I'm bound to reveal there's more to it than that. Feiffer, like so many before him, has overlooked a most significant factor: The Canadian *psyche*.

Yes. Superman was conceived by Toronto-born Joe Shuster who originally worked not for the Daily Planet but for a newspaper called The Star, modelled on the Toronto *Star*. This makes his assumed identity of bland Clark Kent not merely understandable, but artistically inevitable. Kent is the archetypal middle-class Canadian WASP, superficially nice, self-effacing, but within whom there burns a hate-ball, a would-be avenger with superhuman powers, a smasher of bridges, a breaker of skyscrapers, a potential ravager of wonder women. And (may those who have scoffed at Canadian culture in the past, please take note) a universal hero. Superman, first drawn by Shuster in 1938, now appears in twenty languages. This spring, God willing, Lois Lane, who has pined for him all these years, will be married off to a reformed mad scientist, Dr. Lex Luther. I am indebted to another *afficionado*, Alexander Ross, a *Macleans* editor, for all this information. Last March Ross went to visit Joe Shuster, fifty and still single ('I have never met a girl who matched up to Lois Lane,' he has said), at Forest Hills, Long Island, where he lives with his aged mother. Shuster, sadly, never did own the rights on his creation. It is the property of NPP, who say that by 1948 the legendary Shuster was no longer able to draw the strip because of failing eyesight. He was discharged and now earns a living of sorts as a free-lance cartoonist. 'He is trying', Ross writes, 'to paint pop art – serious comic strips – and hopes eventually to promote a one-man show in some chic Manhattan gallery.' Such, Ross might have added, is the inevitable fate of the artistic innovator under capitalism.

If Superman, written and drawn by a hard-faced committee with 20–20 vision these days, continues to flourish, so do the imitations; and here it is worth noting how uncomfortably the parodies of the anarchistic left and broad Jewish humour have come to resemble the earnestly-meant propaganda of the lunatic right.

On the left, *The Realist* has for some time now been running a comic strip about Leroi Jones called Supercoon. Little Leroi becomes mighty Supercoon, threat to the virtue of white women everywhere, by uttering the magic curse,

'Mother-fucker'. Jones, I'm told, was so taken with this parody that he wrote the script for an animated cartoon called Supercoon which he wished to have made and released with the film version of his play *Dutchman*. It has, however, yet to be produced. On a more inane level, *Kosher Comics*, a one-shot parody, published in New York, which runs strips called The Lone Arranger (with the masked marriage broker and Tante), Tishman of the Apes, and Dick Shamus, also includes Supermax, who is called upon to defeat invaders from the planet Blech. The invaders are crazy for matzoh balls.

Meanwhile, back at American Nazi headquarters in Arlington, Va., the *Stormtrooper* magazine has recently given us Whiteman. 'Jew Commies Tremble . . . Nigger Criminals Quake In Fear . . . Liberals Head For The Hills . . . Here Comes Whiteman.' In his first adventure, Whiteman, whose costume is a duplicate of Supey's, except that the emblem on his chest is a swastika rather than an S, 'fights an interplanetary duel with a diabolical fiend. . . . THE JEW FROM OUTER SPACE.' He also does battle with SUPERCOON. In real life, Whiteman is a milkman named Lew Cor (Rockwell spelt backwards, for Nazi Commander George Lincoln Rockwell) and is transformed into Whiteman by speaking the secret words, 'Lieh Geis!' 'With my super-vision,' Whiteman says, 'I can see three niggers have been caught in the act of trying to burn down a Negro church. If they had not been caught in the act, some poor southern white man would have been blamed for it.' He soon beats up the Negro arsonists ('Sweet dreams, Jigaboo.'), but meanwhile, inside a mysterious spacecraft, MIGHTY MOTZA is creating SUPERCOON with an atomic reverse-ray gun. The emblem on Supercoon's chest, incidentally, is a half-peeled banana, and naturally he is no match for Whiteman, who quickly eliminates him. 'So long, Supercoon! You just couldn't make the grade with your second-class brain. With my white man intelligence, I have reduced you to a super-revolting protoplasmic slime. Ugh! Looks like a vile jellyfish.'

In the past, comic strips, or derivatives thereof, have been put to less extreme political purpose. All of us, I'm sure, remember the late Vicky's Supermac. Parralax, publishers of *Kosher Comics*, have also brought out *Great Society Comics*, with Super LBJ and Wonderbird; and *Bobman and Teddy Comics*, featuring the Kennedy brothers. Then day by day, in the Paris edition of *New York Herald Tribune*, *Washington Post* and hundreds of other newspapers, Steve Canyon and Buzz Sawyer risk their lives for us in Vietnam. Canyon, a more politically-conscious type than Sawyer, has recently had some sour things to say about dove-like congressmen and student peace-niks: neither fighter has yet had anything to say about Whiteman. If and when the crunch comes on the Mekong Delta, it remains an open question whether or not Buzz and Steve would accept Whiteman's support.

Canyon's political past, incidentally, is not unblemished. When he came to serve at a u.s. Air Force base in northern Canada in 1960, the Peterborough, Ont., *Examiner* took umbrage. 'We have become disturbed by the political implications of the strip. The hero and his friends were on what was obviously Canadian soil, but it seemed to be entirely under the domination of American troops who were there as a first-line defence against the Russians.' There was only one manly answer possible: Canadian-made strips such as Larry Brannon, a non-starter, who was to glamourize the face of Canada. In his first adventure, Brannon visited 'Toronto, focus of the future, channel for the untold wealth of the north, communications centre of a vast, rich hinterland, metropolis of rare and precious metals'. The last time we were asked to make do with Canadian comics was during the war years when in order to protect *our* balance of payments the government stopped the import of American comic books. The Canadian comic books hastily published to fill the gap were simply awful. We wouldn't have them. Banning American comic books was a typically unimaginative measure, for whatever pittance the government made up in U.S. currency, it lost in home front morale. Comics, as Feiffer has written, were our junk. Our fix. And before long a street corner black market in *Detectice* and *Action* comics began to flourish. Just as we had come to the support of Americans during the prohibition years, thereby founding more than one Canadian family fortune, so the Americans now saw that we didn't go without. Customs barriers erected against a free exchange of ideas never work.

I have no quarrel with Feiffer's selection from the comics for his *The Great Comic Book Heroes*, but his text, the grammar and punctuation quirky, seemed to me somewhat thin. Feiffer is most knowledgeable, a veritable Rashi, on the origins and history of the comic books. He is at his most absorbing when he writes about his own experience as a comic book artist. He learned to draw in the schlock houses, the art schools of the business. 'We were a generation,' he writes. 'We thought of ourselves the way the men who began the movies must have.' And indeed they went to see *Citizen Kane* again and again, to study Welles's use of angle shots. Rumours spread that Welles in his turn had read and learned from the comic books. Fellini was certainly a devotee.

In the schlock houses, Feiffer writes, 'Artists sat lumped in crowded rooms, knocking it out for a page rate. Pencilling, inking, lettering in the balloons for ten dollars a page, sometimes less. . . .'; decadence setting in during the war. The best men, Feiffer writes, went off to fight, hacks sprouting up everywhere. 'The business stopped being thought of as a life's work and became a stepping stone. Five years in it at best, then on to better things: a daily strip, or illustrating for the *Saturday Evening Post*, or getting a job with an advertising agency. . . . By the end of the war, the men who had been colouring our childhood fantasies had become archetypes of the grown-ups who made us need to have fantasies in the first place.

But it was Dr. Wertham, with his *Seduction Of The Innocent*, who really brought an end to an era. His book led to the formation of a busybody review board and an insufferable code that amounted to the emasculation of comic books as we had known them.

1. Respect for parents, the moral code, and for honourable behaviour, shall be fostered.
2. Policemen, judges, government officials and respected institutions shall never be presented in such a way as to create disrespect for established authority.
3. In every instance, good shall triumph over evil and the criminal punished for his misdeeds.

To be fair, there were uplifting, mind-improving side-effects. Culture came to the news stands in the shape of *True Comics*, *Bible Comics*, and the unforgettable series of *Classic Comics* from which Feiffer quotes the death scene from Hamlet.

> Fear not, queen mother!
> It was Laertes
> And he shall die at my hands!
> . . . Alas! I have been poisoned
> And now I, too go
> To join my deceased father!
> I, too – I – AGGGRRRAA!

Today, men in their thirties and forties trade old comic books with other addicts and buy first issues of *Superman* and *Batman* for fifty dollars or more. Although the original boyhood appeal of the comic books was all but irresistible to my generation, I have not gone into the reasons until now for they seemed to me obvious. *Superman, The Flash, The Human Torch,* even *Captain Marvel, were* our *golems*. They were invulnerable, all-conquering, whereas we were puny, miserable, and defeated. They were also infinitely more reliable than real-life champions. Max Schmeling could take Joe Louis. Mickey Owen might drop that third strike. The Nazi Rats could bypass the Maginot Line, and the Yellow-Belly Japs could take Singapore, but neither dared mix it up with Captain America, the original John Bircher, endlessly decorated by FBI head J. Arthur Grover, and sponsor of the Sentinels of Liberty, to which we could all belong (regardless of race, colour or creed) by sending a dime to Timely Publications, 330 West 42nd St., N.Y., and signing a pledge (the original loyalty oath?) that read: 'I solemnly pledge to uphold the principals of the Sentinels of Liberty and assist Captain America in his war against spies in the U.S.A.'

Finally, many of our heroes were made of paltry stuff. The World's Mightiest Man, Powerful Champion of Justice, Captain Marvel was mere Billy Batson, newsboy, until he uttered the magic word, 'Shazam!' The Flash is another case in point.

> 'Faster than the streak of lightning in the sky . . . Swifter than the speed of light itself . . . Fleeter than the rapidity of thought . . . is *The Flash*, reincarnation of the winged Mercury . . . His speed is the dismay of scientists, the joy of the oppressed – And the open mouthed wonder of the multitudes!'

Originally however he was as weak as you or I. A decidedly forlorn figure. He was Jay Garrick, 'an unknown student at a mid-western university . . .' and, for my money, a Jew. The creators of *The Flash*, Gardner Fox and Harry Lampert even like Arthur Miller, wrote at a time, remember, when Jews were still thinly disguised as Gentiles on the stage, in novels, and comic books. There is no doubt, for instance, that *The Green Lantern* has its origin in Hassidic mythology. Will Eisner's *The Spirit*, so much admired by Feiffer, is given to cabalistic superstitions and speaking in parables. With *The Flash*, however, we are on the brink of a new era, a liberated era. Jay Garrick is Jewish, but Reform. Semi-assimilated. In the opening frame, lovely Joan (significantly blonde) won't date him, because he is only a scrub on the university football team while Bull Tyron is already a captain. 'A man of your build and brains', she says, 'could be a star. . . . A scrub is just an old washwoman! You won't put your mind to football. . . !' Jay, naturally, is intellectually inclined. Probably he is taking freshman English with Leslie Fiedler. An eye-opener! Huck Finn and Nigger Jim, like Batman and Robin, are fags. Jay, however, spends most of the time in the lab with his professor. Then one day an experiment with hard water goes 'Wrong'. Jay, overcome by fumes, lurches forward. ('It's . . . it's . . . too much for me. . . .') He lies between life and death for weeks, coming out of it endowed with superhuman powers. 'Science', the doctor explains, 'knows that hard water makes a person act much quicker than ordinarily. . . . By an intake of its gases, Jay can walk, talk, run and think swifter than thought. . . . He will probably be able to outrace a bullet!! He is a freak of science!' Briefly, he is now The Flash.

How puerile, how unimaginative, today's comic strips seem by comparison. Take Rex Morgan, M.D., for instance. In my day, to be a doctor was to be surrounded by hissing test tubes and vile green gases. It was to be either a cackling villain with a secret formula that would reduce Gotham City to the size of a postage stamp or to be a noble genius, creator of behemoths who would bring hope to the oppressed multitudes. The best that can be expected of the loquacious Dr. Morgan is that he will lecture us on the hidden dangers of medicare. Or save a student from LSD addiction. There's no magic in him. He's commonplace. A bore.

Once, it was ruled that any serious novelist or playwright who tried his hand at film-writing was a sellout. Indeed, many a novelist-turned-screenwriter next proffered a self-justifying, lid-lifting novel about Hollywood, wherein the most masculine stars were surreptitiously (not to say gratifyingly) queer, the most glamorous girls were empty inside, deep inside, but lo and behold, the writer, on the last page, had left the dream palace, fresh winds rippling through his untamed hair, to write the book-of-the-month you had just finished reading. Later, the novelist returned to Hollywood, but *on his own terms*, to do the screenplay of his novel. It was filmed frankly, outspokenly, and everybody felt better inside, deep inside.

Hollywood is one thing, London another. No better than the archetypal boss's son, I started out at the bottom in films. I got work as a reader for a studio script department. For two quid, in 1955, a reader was expected to write a ten page synopsis of a book followed by a shrewd evaluation of its film potential. Like Harold Robbin's visual, but Proust isn't. Experts, I discovered, managed to zip through and report on as many as four books a day. I never got to be an expert. One day a script editor handed me a book for which, she said, I would be paid a double fee. It was Brecht's *Mother Courage*. 'The play's only sixty pages,' I said. 'Why can't the producer read it himself?'

I did not yet know that it was no more expected of most producers to actually read books than it was, say, of Walter O'Malley to chop down trees to make baseball bats. So I took the play home, wrote a synopsis, and mailed it off. The next morning the script editor phoned me, outraged. 'But you haven't said whether or not you think it would make a good film,' she said.

That ended my career as a reader, but shortly afterwards I was hired to write a script for the TV serial mill. The hero of the series was a freelance sea captain (tough, fearless, jaunty), and my script took him to Spain for some smuggling. The producer didn't like it one bit. 'You call this a script? What's this here? Two guys talking. *Talking*? Yak-yak-yak for two whole pages. Where's the action?'

I bought a book with three screenplays in it by Graham Greene and set to work again. I made absolutely no plot or dialogue changes, but, whereas a page of my first draft script read,

CARLOS: Things are very quiet here tonight. I do not like it, Nick.
NICK: I was just wondering . . .

my revised, professional version read,

CARLOS: Things are very quiet here tonight. I do not like it, Nick.
SOUND: *It is very quiet.*
   ≪CUT TO CU NICK. *He lights a cigarette. He inhales.*≫
NICK: ≪with a far-off, wondering look≫ I was just wondering . . .

I had arrived. Another writer, hired to do two half-hour comedies, pilots for a possible series for Peter Sellers (Sellers, at the time, had made only one feature-length film, *The Lady Killers*), made me his collaborator. He wanted company. He executed all the routines meant for Sellers. I learned to say, 'Why, that's swell. A great gag.' I did the typing and brewed the tea. Eventually, we were summoned to a script conference. Present were Sellers, the director, the producer, two assistants, my collaborator, and I. We sat solemnly round an enormous table in a board room overlooking Hyde Park. Before each of us there was a pad, a pencil, and a glass of water. The producer, a tiny wizened man with pebble-glasses, told us, 'Gentlemen, we are here to exchange ideas. To my right is our director. Need I say, a *great* talent. A talent I have engaged, I might say, for a pretty penny.'

The director, who hadn't worked in years, said 'I consider this series a challenge.'

The rest of us were fulsomely introduced. 'Now about the script. . . .' Squinting, the producer held the script no more than two inches from his face. 'Page twenty-nine, boys. We've slowed down here. We need a gimmick. Well, if you saw *Love Happy* with the Marx Brothers you will recall there was a great scene in that picture. Harpo is leaning against a wall. Groucho comes by and says, what are you doing, holding up the building? Harpo nods. He moves away and the building collapses.'

Sellers was silent.

'Now, boys, ours is a small budget film. What I think we could do on page twenty-nine is this. Instead of a building Mr. Sellers could be leaning against a lamp post. When he moves away,' the producer said, already beginning to break up with laughter, 'the lamp post falls down.'

Sellers lit one cigarette off another.

'Page thirty-two, boys. Have you ever had the good fortune to see Mr. Danny Kaye, a great comedian, in *Up in Arms*'?

To my astonishment, the two films were made and distributed. I never saw them, but within months I was working on my first feature film, a mediocre thriller that required rewrites. The director wasn't jumpy, he was panic-stricken, and he insisted that I work with him at his flat every day. Together we raked each scene over and over again.

'Mn,' he'd say, reading a page just ripped out of the typewriter, 'jolly good. . . . Well, not bad. But would he say *that*?

Is it really in character for him to say "thank you" at that moment?'

I'd look pensive. Wearily I'd say, 'I think you're on to something, you know. It *is* out of character. I think he'd say "thanks", not "thank you".'

'But isn't that too American-y?'

'Exactly. But that's the point. *He's American-oriented.*'

The director sometimes kept me all day without doing any writing. Nervously, he would dig out his copy of *Spotlight*, a catalogue with photographs of almost every actor and actress in the country, and solicit my opinion on casting. My opinion was worthless and, if you figured it at a day's pay, worthless *and* expensive.

'What would you think of John Mills?'

'He's all right.'

'What do you mean all right? Are you holding something back? Do you know something?'

I swore I didn't.

'What about Jack Hawkins?'

'Sure.'

'If you don't like Jack Hawkins, tell me. This is very important.'

Like most novelists, I am conditioned to working for months on material I discuss with nobody, because to talk about it is to risk losing it. To adjust from that to script writing, where you are bound to meet once a week with a director or producer or both to discuss work in shaky first-draft form and work yet to be done, is more than unnerving, it's indecent. It is too much like what Truman Capote once described as group sports.

Here it is necessary to make a sharp distinction between the entertainment and the so-called art film, each presenting the novelist-turned-scriptwriter with special problems. I'd like to deal with the entertainment first because it's simpler, a straightforward street corner deal. Money is time, and writing an entertainment can buy a novelist a very sweet chunk of it.

As a general rule, the writer who adapts a thriller or a bestseller for the screen is the most lowly and expendable of technicians; in fact most take-charge, can-do producers don't feel secure until they've hired and fired one writer after another, licking the script into shape, as they say. Once I was summoned by a producer who had already hired a writer for an adventure film he was going to make. Although the writer had not yet begun work, the producer wanted to know if I could take over within twelve weeks. 'What', I asked, 'if the man you've got turns in a script that doesn't require more work?'

'Don't worry,' the producer replied immediately, 'he can only go seven innings.'

Traditionally, producers are the butt of most film jokes, but in my limited dealings I've found many of them engaging and surprisingly forthright about their needs. At the moment, too, they are running touchingly scared. Commercial producers are baffled by the new films, they don't understand their success. Arty directors, writers, and actors, whom the big production units have been shunning for years, are not only making pix but some of their pix are making money. Wowsy in Denver, boffo in Cincy. Suddenly art is good biz. So now the call is out for no-saying playwrights, black humorists, and dirty-minded novelists. Only the producers still want the same old stuff, the good old stuff, but tarted up, modishly done, with frozen frames, action speeded up here, slowed down there, clichés shot through a brandy glass or as seen reflected in a cat's eye, and performers talking directly to the audience. It's much as if, instead of printing the best take, they've now begun to print the take before the last, the one wherein the actors sent up the film, including jokes that were hitherto private, limited to the studio unit. Which, incidentally, often brings the bewildered producers full circle, right back to where many of them started out years and years ago, making Robert Benchley and Edgar Kennedy shorts.

The problems involved in writing a screenplay for a seriously meant film are at once more intricate and perplexing, assuming that you are adapting somebody else's novel or play. To begin with, there's your relationship with the director. A talented director does not eat a batch of interchangeable writers; he seeks out, and is prepared to wait for, the writer he wants and who, he feels, will see a screenplay through from beginning to end. He will treat a writer well, protecting him from prying, nervy producers, stars who want a peek at the script-in-progress, and other occupational hazards; but in return he demands that you do your best for him. Let me put it another way. He has actually read your novels, not your screenplays, and that's why he wants you.

Flattering. But how far do you go with such a director? How many of your own original ideas do you contribute to an adaptation of somebody else's work? I have, for instance, twice worked for Jack Clayton, on the final script for *Room At The Top* and doing the screenplay for John Le Carre's *The Looking Glass War*. I've also worked with Ted Kotcheff, writing the screenplay for *Life At The Top*. In each case, as a novelist myself, with split loyalties, I couldn't help feeling that no matter what I added to Braine or Le Carre the written work remained essentially theirs, justifiably so. Why, then, do more than adapt? Why turn in a scene or an idea or a character you've been hoarding and can very nicely use in one of your own novels?

Ideally, I used to believe the thing would be to get yourself commissioned to write an original screenplay, but I no longer think so, if only because even under the most ideal circumstances film is not a writer's medium. Film-making belongs more than anything to the writer-director, say

Fellini, and, failing that, to the truly gifted director, always remembering that the director, no matter how inspired, who cannot write his own scripts is an incomplete artist.

One comes away from film-making with an increasing respect for the serious director, one who needs somebody else for the script. I speak here of the director who will not make any film, even any worthwhile film, unless it touches him. To watch him between films, devouring novels and plays, reading scripts, is to witness the anguish of a sadly dependent man. Why wait for novels or plays, then, why not get something of his own going? Sometimes he does, but the sort of writer such a director would like to commission to write an original screenplay is also the kind who presents the most difficulties. In the nature of things, he won't or can't submit an idiotic four-page synopsis to be sent on to a producer for financing. More seriously, he is loath to write an original screenplay because his ego, like the director's, tends to be discomfitingly large, and the same concept committed to a novel remains in his control.

Even given an admirable screenplay, my sympathies remain with the director. The writer leads a comparatively sheltered life, everything happens in his room. The director, equally proud and sensitive, if you like, is almost always on. Performing. Not only must he be able to con producers and flatter actors, but, ultimately, he has to be up to making his mistakes in public. The writer, having done a scene badly, rips it out of his typewriter and tries again or goes out to shoot pool for the rest of the day. Nobody knows. The director, botching a scene, does it before a crowd. His off-days are shared and possibly savoured by an entire studio unit and there may not be time or money left to re-do the scene.

As recently as 1962, Daniel Fuchs was driven to defending his abandoning fiction for the movies. 'Generations to come,' he wrote in *Commentary*, 'looking back over the years, are bound to find that the best, the most solid creative effort of our decades was spent in the movies, and it's time someone came clean and said so.'

Today no apologies are asked for or given. The movies have become increasingly, almost insufferably modish, especially among writers, intellectuals and students. In fact, the sort of student who once used to help put out a little magazine is nowadays more likely to be making a movie with a hand-held camera. His mentors are Antonioni, Resnais, Godard, Losey, Bergman, Fellini, Polanski, etc. He also studies corny old movies, resuscitated as camp.

This is not to say that in our student days, in the Forties, we did not cut morning lectures to watch the Marx Brothers or guffaw at inspirational war films. Say, *The Pride of the Marines* with John Garfield. In an early scene, as I recall it, Garfield has a Jap grenade explode smack in his face, but he continues to fire his machine gun heroically with Dane Clark's help. Shipped back to a military hospital in San Francisco, blinded but unscarred(!), Garfield dictates a letter to his sweetheart saying he never wants to see her again, he's found somebody else. The truth is Garfield is too proud to become a burden to such a nice girl as Eleanor Parker. He tells Dane Clark bitterly, 'Nobody will give a blind man a job,' and Clark replies, if I remember correctly, '*I've* always had that problem. My name is Shapiro.'

This era of treacly, brother-loving films, in which so many of the good guys were Jews or Negroes and nearly all the shits were WASPS, broke up with the coming of McCarthyism. Ultimately Senator McCarthy – so despicable in his time, seen to be such a buffoon in retrospect – may come to be appreciated as the most effective of cultural brooms. He did more than *Cahiers du Cinema* or *Sight & Sound* to clean the liberal hacks as well as some talented men out of Hollywood.

But the point I was really trying to make here was that we,

too, laughed at jingoism, bad taste, and enjoyed slapstick: however, as we took this to be altogether unexceptionable, we did not go on and on about it. We did not enshrine it. calling it camp. I should add, incidentally, that we also went in for screwing in the afternoon. Or, as a thought-provoking *Time* essayist might put it, we had sex without love. But we did not think for a minute that this made us revolutionaries. Or alienated. Or that it was happening for the first time. We put it down to being horny, that's all.

I throw this in because so much that is praised in the new, serious films is dependent on an appallingly ignorant, mistaken belief that things *are* happening for the first time. The truth is they are only happening for the first time on film. But I'll return to this later. First I'd like to deal with camp.

Camp, the old Batman serials revived, Randolph Scott Westerns, need not detain us long. In passing, however, I must say one can only pity the American middle class. Excoriated by a generation of novelists for being Babbitts, jeered at for years for preferring the Andrew Sisters to Vivaldi, A. J. Cronin to Marcel Proust, and Norman Rockwell to Picasso, they are now being howled at for giving in. While they were doing their cultural home-work (going to listen to John Mason Brown when he was in town, gobbling up Clifton Fadiman anthologies), Vivaldi, Picasso, and Proust have gone out of style. Artists, sensing encirclement by a middle class with a newly found leisure time, have abandoned that space on the cultural board, pronouncing it square, and scampered round to attack sneakily from the rear. Now they are telling the striving middle class that there is nothing to beat the crap the self-improvers left behind them.

Well, I, too, can enjoy Monogram Pictures and other old trash, in limited quantities, but I strongly object to the new sub-literature on old pop films, if only because it is so awesomely serious and self-inflated. A case in point is *An Illustrated History of Horror Films* by Carlos Clarens, wherein the author writes, 'Unlike the Western, the horror film has not attracted sufficient critical attention. . . . What seems to put the reviewers off horror films, what prevents them from surrendering their critical resistance, is the frequent – and necessary – depiction of the fantastic. But do we dismiss a painting by Fra Angelico or Max Ernst because we don't, simply won't, believe in angels and sphinxes? Is it indispensable that one be a Christian to read Saint John in Patmos?' This shaky, utterly unacceptable analogy is, I'm afraid, typical of the 'critical attention' Mr. Clarens and others focus on a thin subject. Elsewhere, Mr. Clarens is obvious or superficial. 'A supremely violent age like ours', he writes, 'calls for an unprecedented violence in its aesthetic manifestations. . . .' But the violence of horror films is not of this age at all, but dependent on the vampire and other myths of a much earlier age and the gothic novels and ghost stories of a time we have come to look back on as enviably more secure than ours.

There are two opposite, but equally tiresome, equally humourless, ways to approach the subject of horror films: to condemn them as harmful to children, as Dr. Frederic Wertham does in his book, *Seduction of the Innocent;* or, like the unblinking Carlos Clarens, to unearth in them 'hidden' sexual meanings (driving stakes into beautiful, bosomy blondes?), a necessary release, catharsis.

Mr. Clarens's History, in common with so many other books of film criticism, is more of a catalogue than an illumination: it bulges with lists of titles and credits, plot synopsis spilling over plot synopsis. Here, for instance, you may, discover that *Abbott and Costello Meet Dr. Jekyll and Mr. Hyde* was made by Universal in 1953, directed by Charles Lamonte written by Leo Leob and John Grant, photographed by George Robinson, and among the cast were Craig Stevens, John Dierkes, and Reginald Denny. *Red Planet Mars*, on the other hand, was made in 1952 by United Artists-Veiller-

Hyde, directed by Harry Horner, with music by David Chudnow, and a cast that included Morris Ankrum, House Peters, and Gene Roth. . . . Such incriminating information should, perhaps, more decently be limited to friends, very good friends, and agents, but if you want it, here it is.

The main point about horror, however, is that it is more suited to literature than film, for the truly horrifying is the unseen. Monsters from outer space, vampires, cat women, Frankensteins, and zombies scare us only so long as they are off screen. Once perceived, they are comic or endearing. King Kong, for example, was a honey. The film made of King Kong was *technically* brilliant, but it is Mr. Clarens's error, shared with too many other writers on film, to confuse special effects, cutting-room wizardry, and other mechanical advances, with art.

The sometimes stupefying, but undeniably formative, effect years of movie-going has had on all of us has yielded at least one good comic novel, Walker Percy's *The Moviegoer*, and, more recently, what I take to be a trend-setting film, *Morgan*, wherein the hero – no, no, the anti-hero – identifies with King Kong and Tarzan.

Morgan, the work of an intelligent director and a talented writer, Karel Reisz and David Mercer respectively, was occasionally very funny indeed. It introduced Vanessa Redgrave to moviegoers, something we should all be grateful for. But the film's underlying premise was surprisingly reactionary and could not but fortify smug middlebrow clichés about the artist. Morgan is endearing, outrageous, cute, inventive, but essentially a child, an intellectual Dagwood, dependent on his wife, unable to manage his own affairs, and clearly too kooky to pronounce on politics. None of Morgan's declared fantasies are as worrying as the unspoken daydream, integral to his character, that the working-class artist is such a lovable child that the girl-with-the-Rolls-

Royce, should she only meet him, would find him irresistible and take care of him for evermore. Then in *Morgan*, as in other new films, there has been a curious displacement. In earlier serious cinema, say *Brief Encounter*, the working class was introduced as comic relief. In *Morgan* it is the middle class that is used to do the funny bits between. There has been no broadening of vision; rather, a change in focus.

This change in focus can be traced back to *Room At The Top*, generally agreed to be such a breakthrough in British film-making. Like so many cinema breakthroughs, however, it was actually a reverberation of a literary eruption.

In 1955 the last of the British colonies, the indigenous working class, rebelled again, this time demanding not free medical care and pension schemes, already torn from the state by their elders, but a commanding voice in the arts and letters. Briefly, a new style in architecture.

At its best, this gave us Alan Sillitoe and, at its most hilarious, a reputable publisher's ad promising a new book with 'all grammatical errors intact, not one spelling mistake corrected'. We were also offered Braine, Wesker, Delaney, Colin Wilson and, above all, Joan Littlewood.

I come from a continent justly accused, I think, of having often confused vitality with art, but in England, for a while, it seemed to be a new rule. Joan Littlewood was a case in point.

To begin with, there was the schmaltzy, romantic notion that a working-class district would support a theatre that truly reflected the conditions of its own life. One, to my way of looking, the Theatre Workshop never did reflect these conditions truthfully, and two, to make the long dreary trip out to Stratford East was to see all your Hampstead, Swiss Cottage, and even Chelsea friends. Most of the young working-class boys I did see at the Theatre Royal came, it seemed to me in exactly the same spirit as I used to go to the theatre when I was a boy, that is to see some 'hot stuff'. Miss Littlewood –

shrewdly, I think – did not disappoint. What I saw at the Theatre Royal was plenty of vitality as well as the most boorish, reactionary attitudes remembered from my childhood. By this token, to present an artist on stage is to reveal an outlandish queer (the interior decorator in *Fings Ain't Wot They Used t' Be*); the poor are warm, funny, and hate the middle class; and, turning a West End cliché on its head, the panty straps of all the girls of Kensington Gore melt at the thought of a navvy's hot hand.

This somewhat condescending, decidedly romantic interpretation of the working class infected *Room At The Top*, the breakthrough film, and the spate of 'frank, outspoken' films that followed. *Saturday Night and Sunday Morning*, *A Taste of Honey*, *A Kind of Loving*, etc. etc. Six years after Jack Clayton's *Room At The Top*, in 1964, the same story was retold as comedy for the first time in *Nothing But The Best*, a bridging film that prepared us for *Morgan* and *Georgy Girl*.

In *Room At The Top*, a gritty venture, Joe Lampton (out of Balzac by way of Dreiser) had to choose between love and money, and when he opted for the latter, a moral judgement was implied. Joe had become corrupt and for this he would suffer. In *Nothing But The Best*, Jimmy Brewster, a real estate clerk with a lower middle-class background, has made his choice before the picture even begins. He's corrupt, but *gleefully* corrupt. He will not suffer soulfully for it in later life because, let's face it, we all stink. Brewster is Lampton looked at through another, more contemporary, lens. While *Room At The Top* sprang from a climate of anger, Osborne, Suez and CND, *Nothing But The Best* was typical of another wind of change. It came after *Beyond The Fringe*, through *TW3* and *Private Eye* and the James Bond books.

If Lampton reaches the top by marrying the boss's daughter, he is filled with anguish at the wedding because he feels responsible for the suicide of his mistress. Brewster, who has also married into wealth, feels no such remorse because he has been obliged to murder his brother-in-law en route. All that worries him is the possibility of his crime being inconveniently discovered. With *Morgan*, we move beyond guilt or even practical fears. He, too, has found freedom by marrying a rich girl, but in a world where everybody's insane, it's the lunatic who is the sainted child. Nothing bothers Morgan.

Yet *Morgan*, whatever its shortcomings, was not without wit and did not insult the intelligence. It is clearly one of those films meant, when we hear it argued, as I imagine we have all heard it argued, that films have finally displaced the novel. To some extent, this is true. Fellini's *I Vitelloni* was not only first-rate, but a new departure. For the first time, as far as I know, a conventional first novel (young man, disgusted with values of a provincial town, leaves for the capital) was not written but instead brilliantly composed for film.

In recent years, it is fair to say that films have become less juvenile, more intelligent. An increasing number of good satisfying films have come from Europe. There have been two or three that are arguably great. But, by and large, I am convinced that the new films are not nearly so good as they are cracked up to be, their seriousness is often spurious and half-educated, and they are being critically oversold. A major trouble is we are so grateful for even a modicum of originality on the screen, we are so flattered to be addressed directly, we seldom realize that the so-called serious film is, for the most part, shamelessly derivative, taking up a position abandoned by novelists years ago.

Meanwhile, film reviewers continue to gush. Unmissable! Electrifying! Breath-taking! Beautiful! Once-in-a-lifetime! One of those rare. . . .! Raw with genius! To open up a London or New York newspaper at the cinema pages is to discover masterpieces held over for the third month everywhere. Film masterpieces are minted at least twice a month. No other art form, as they say, can make that claim. However, it is equally true that the masterpieces in no other art form are so relentlessly up-to-date. Or date so quickly.

Before turning to consider a recent masterpiece, *Blow-Up*, it might be instructive to recall that *Brief Encounter* was once hailed as a breakthrough. So, come to think of it, was *The Best Years of Our Lives*. They seemed frank and outspoken in their sociological time, just as more recent masterpieces pull no punches in our infinitely more sizzling, sexy time.

Ads for *Blow-Up* pointedly exploited sex. They showed Vanessa Redgrave stripped to the waist, arms crossed over her breasts. 'Antonioni's camera', the copy ran, 'never flinches. At love without meaning. At murder without guilt. At the dazzle and the madness of London today. SHE'S DARING! EXCITING! PROVOCATIVE IN. . . .'

Cut the cake any way you like. Modern life is empty, experience is meaningless, sex deadening, but when we lined up for *Blow-Up* we knew, in our hearts, exactly what we hoped to see. A tit show. Not only that. In the scene where the anti-hero romps with two nude girls on his studio floor, there was supposed to be a crotch shot, pubic hairs that would not titillate but were indicative of our spiritual malaise, the sick times we live in, etc. etc. etc.

In these heady, permissive times, the movies have it all over your adult sex novel. The four-letter words, all spelled the same, soon pall on us, not so the breasts and private parts of stars and starlets, especially when we can ogle in the name of art, with no guilt attached, as there would be coming out into the sun after an afternoon at the nudies.

The fact is a number of so-called serious film directors have been able to con the censor, getting away with a good deal of windy talk on the subject of sex as a profound comment on our Godless time, when it is merely salacious. Not that I'm against nudity in films; it gives me a charge. Why, I am even grateful that the orgy scene has become as integral a part of so many adult films (*La Dolce Vita*, *Darling*, *The Loved One*) as freckled kids and dogs with wagging tails were to Walt Disney. What I do object to is the hot stuff going by another name.

Sydney Lumet, for instance, was able to argue successfully for a bare-breasted shot of a coloured prostitute in his ponderous, prosaic *The Pawnbroker*, claiming high purpose and, incidentally, acquiring a lot of useful publicity. Most likely, Lumet believed the shot necessary to the film, just as he obviously considered it powerful stuff to show a nude, sexy Jewish wife waiting for her SS man on her concentration camp bed. If so, he is a man of integrity who suffers, alas, from a failure of taste and imagination.

In any event, I would give a lot to sit with Jack Valenti and his bunch, or the Catholic Legion of Decency, as they deliberate – loftily, I'm sure – on whose breasts are edifying, whose lascivious. On their curious, decidedly prudish scale of values, I rather imagine Ingrid Bergman's breasts are the cleanest, whereas Raquel Welch's big boobs would come at the bottom of the scale, the very nipples being dirty-minded.

Anyway, *Blow-Up*, unflinching camera and all, promises rather more than it fulfils. Miss Redgrave, in her big scene, does cavort bare to the waist, arms uncrossed, but she always has her broad back to us. Like the supposedly torrid paperbacks of my high school days, *Blow-Up* is a tease. This is fair comment because Antonioni's film is not a flawed work of art, which would command respect, but a good commercial idea, badly realized.

The good commercial idea buried within *Blow-Up* is also its only plot thread. An immensely rich and successful photographer (David Hemmings), wandering through a London park one day, begins to snap pictures of a girl (Vanessa Redgrave) and a man romping lyrically in the distance. The girl urgently demands the film. He refuses. She goes so far as to visit his studio and offer to sleep with him. His curiosity aroused, the photographer develops the film and notices an ambiguous blur in the bushes. In *Blow-Up's* central sequence he enlarges this area of the print again and again, until he thinks he can identify a dead body. Has he seen a murder? The photographer returns to the park and finds the body still lying there. Back at his studio, however, he discovers that his enlargements have been stolen. At the park once more, he discovers that the body has now disappeared as well. Has he seen a murder or not? Is what we – any of us – see, true?

Within this modish framework, Antonioni has contrived to tip his modish hat at most, if not all, 'cool' concerns. The Bomb. Pot. Alienation. Queers. And joyless sexual connections, if, that is, you are willing to accept that for a young bachelor to make love to two pretty young girls on his studio floor is more *Angst*-ridden than fun-filled.

The thin plot aside, everything else in *Blow-Up*, the sequence of other events, follows an arbitrary pattern. If a fragmentary meeting in a restaurant comes after a modelling scene, then the order of the two scenes could just as easily be reversed. Sensational experiences wash over our anti-hero, but being uninvolved or cool, he never gets wet. Neither, come to think of it, does he act. 'An actor', Antonioni recently said, 'is only *one* element – perhaps sometimes the most important. But the director is the only person who understands the composition. If an actor thinks he understands, he becomes the director himself, which is a great disaster.'

In the same interview, with Francis Wyndham of the London *Sunday Times*, he went on to say:

'Life is irregular – sometimes fast, sometimes slow. It is ridiculous to *impose* a rhythm, as films did before the war: it may be a perfect rhythm, but it is false. Simplicity can have a place in art – but never for its own sake. There are some complicated things in life, and it is a sort of betrayal to simplify them. Today, with scientific progress teaching us to see things in a more subtle way, there is much in the world that we can't explain. We are victims of this problem, this effort to represent them.

Man is complicated. Everything has been tried, studied, analysed, cut into pieces. One could perhaps understand the moon, the universe, even the horizons of life – but man himself remains mysterious. Life is difficult. My films are true.'

Yes, yes, life is irregular, sometimes fast, sometimes slow, but *Blow-Up* struck me as simplified and untrue. It is about attitudes, not people. Antonioni, reacting strongly to a tiresome cliché of adult films (and middlebrow stage plays and novels) of twenty years ago has not moved beyond it: he has inverted it. In the bad old days, for instance, nobody ever did anything in scene B that hadn't been motivated, 'psychologically motivated,' and *signalled!* in scene A. Or, to look at a concrete variation of this hackneyed, mechanical approach, if our adult hero in scene A was shown to be a lousy anti-Semite, we instantly flashed back to his childhood, scene B, wherein Dr. Hymie Hymovitch overcharged his unemployed father. It was once a convention that armed with a Marxist slide rule and Freudian binoculars, there were no more mysteries, all behaviour could be explained, as (to borrow from the stage) in *Death of a Salesman*. This was oversimplified, a distortion. But it is also oversimplified and distorted to say that nothing whatsoever can be explained and all action is unmotivated and therefore meaningless. It is false and in *Blow-Up* it is taken as a licence to improvise capriciously. If God is dead, the director is lawful. Anything goes. Furthermore, we tend at first to believe in Hemming's reactions and behaviour, because we actually see it. Obviously, we do not resist film as sceptically as we do books.

Which brings me to another problem: the film writer's problem. Film writing, even under the most astute director, seldom calls for the highest order of invention. On the contrary. It is usually an invitation to laziness and sleight of hand. In a novel, for example, one really must avoid the banal. I love you, she says, I love you too, he says, simply won't do. Writing for a film, however, one knows that when she (say, Monica Vitti, Julie Christie or Jane Fonda) says, I love you, she will be undoing her bra straps or, already nude, she will set to licking his ear. Then when he (say Belmondo, Michael Caine or Albert Finney) replies, I love you too, his hand will be fondling a breast or running up a leg. Who's listening? Not me, certainly. There's too much that's juicy to look at.

Similarly, stuck on an expositional scene, an obligatory scene, it is cleverness not imagination that's called for. For example, if he is explaining to her, when I was six years old my mother . . . you write into the script that this essentially boring scene should be shot while they are both in the shower or on a ferris wheel or as seen through a jagged mirror with a stripteaser reflected in it.

In recent years there has also been a substitution of art film clichés for entertainment ones, so that if once we knew that a girl who wore pearls and a cashmere twin set (Joan Fontaine, Dorothy McGuire) couldn't be immoral no matter what suspicions aroused by Hitchcock, we now grasp that any girl with a propensity for walking barefoot or in the rain or especially amid falling autumn leaves (Jeanne Moreau, Monica Vitti) can't be all bad. Similarly, David Hemmings, with his mop of curly blond hair, big sensitive eyes, and Carnaby Street clothes, can't be as boorish as his behaviour suggests. Like Belmondo, Finney, and Terence Stamp, he is the anti-hero type. Most films, no matter how supposedly serious, have failed to progress beyond asking us to identify only with the handsome and the lovely, sometimes to the utter ruination of the story, other times to the salvation of a decidedly sordid little tale.

In John Fowles' novel, *The Collector*, for instance, an unattractive young man, a pinched embittered bank clerk, wins the football pools, buys a country house, catches a beautiful girl and makes her his love prisoner. In the film the pinched young man is played by irresistible, beautiful Terence Stamp, and it is no longer credible that his love prisoner would find his advances repugnant. In *Georgy Girl*, on the other hand, we are asked to find engaging a girl who sleeps with her best friend's lover on the night she is having his baby and then marries a man twice her age for money. We find her endearing only because she is played by Lynn Redgrave, who, incidentally, doesn't for a minute, as she says of herself in one scene, look like the wrong end of a bus.

Anti-heroes and heroines may be *unconventionally* handsome or beautiful, but handsome and beautiful they still are. Terence Stamp and David Hemmings, who look uncannily alike, currently filling the dubious office of hipsters' Andy Hardys. Meanwhile love, except as comic relief, between a short fat man and a flat-chested girl is still beyond the limits of the movies.

'Perhaps Londoners won't like it,' Antonioni has said of *Blow-Up*, 'as they see their city in another way. It could be set in Paris or New York without losing truth. But I think London is the best place. Fashion photographers here belong to this moment. And they are without background; one doesn't know where they come from. Like the girl in my film – one never knows anything about her, not even who she is.'

Blow-Up was certainly not set in the London I or my friends know, but a prettified city, a mannered place. One would not object, one would cheer in fact, if it weren't London as say Kafka's *Amerika* wasn't America, but neither does the film capture the essence of . . . well, 'swinging' London, the invention of American magazines in the first place. There wasn't one exterior sequence in the film that wasn't obviously set up and strained at that. If, for example, two queers stroll down the street, walking a poodle, then they are the only two people on the street, and they are not seen in passing: attention is called, not once, but twice, putting them in italics as it were. Elsewhere, passers-by are Africans in colourful robes, or nuns. Again and again, it is the stunning picture, the arresting image, that is of primary importance, just as in a musical. The scenes in *Blow-Up* which had made it such a commercial success are the sexy ones, and though I enjoyed them because they were lingered on, they could not have been lingered on for any valid artistic reason. If *Blow-Up* is a failure, it is a glossy, commercial one, not a work of art gone sadly wrong. Like too many other new 'serious' films – the love scenes, frank and outspoken, the dialogue daring, as compared to earlier films – it flirts with contemporary concerns without having anything fresh to say.

Norman Mailer declared himself a contender five years ago. 'The sour truth', he wrote in *Advertisements for Myself*, 'is that I am imprisoned with a perception which will settle for nothing less than making a revolution in the consciousness of our time.'

Advertisements, on balance, was an unfortunate but crucial book, for it indicated that Mailer, his last two novels brutally handled by some critics, had assumed a risky stance, teetering on a parapet thirty storeys up (like Steve Rojack in *An American Dream*?) between two incompatible camps. The glittering and feverish one of gossip columnists and best-seller charts and the office of a serious writer. At the time, it seemed that he could still fall either way. *Advertisements* was a compulsively readable, but often embarrassing, compilation of stories and articles and gossip which assumed – at its own peril – that we were as absorbed in Mailer as he was in himself. All the same, the book did establish three things.

1. Mailer had the ability, but too much pride and ambition, to follow his first big success with another naturalistic novel, or as he put it, *The Naked And The Dead Go To Japan*.

2. There was a superb short novel in the collection, *The Man Who Studied Yoga*, which suggested that Mailer just might break through, as advertised. In fact, as he and Cassius Clay ridiculed rivals and hustled in pursuit of different championship belts it seemed that it was Clay who was all bluff, but that Mailer might do the trick.

3. Mailer was hooked on a dangerous Hemingway-cum-Jewish problem. Of Hemingway, he wrote,
   'Let any of you decide for yourself how silly would be

A Farewell To Arms or better, *Death In The Afternoon*,
if it had been written by a man who was five-four, had
acne, wore glasses, spoke in a shrill voice or was a
physical coward. That, of course, is an impossible
hypothesis.'

Impossible? Well, Isaac Babel, for one, wore glasses and
looked to be about five-four, yet his stories of the Red
Cavalry were as splendid as, and somewhat less sentimental
than, anything Hemingway ever wrote.

Then there was the two-fisted debut in *The Time Of Her
Time*, an excerpt from a projected novel, of Mailer's prototype
Super-Goy. Sergius O'Shaugnessy, a six foot plus Irishman
('girls and ladies would try me on off-evenings like comparison shoppers to shop the value of their boy friend, lover,
mate or husband against the certified professionalism of
Sergius O'Shaugnessy'), who was a former trapper in Alaska,
chauffeur to gangsters, officer in the Foreign Legion, labour
organizer and analyst . . . and who sounded ominously like
the fantasy of somebody who was five-four, had acne, spoke
in a shrill voice, etc. etc. etc. Anyway, in the sexual main
bout of *The Time Of Her Time*, Sergius takes on a little
Jewish dumpling who hitherto was unable to have an
orgasm and leads her over the mountain by telling her at the
crucial moment, 'You're a dirty little Jew.'

There are, incidentally, two variations on this theme in *An
American Dream*. After murdering his wife, Steve Rojack
opens the door to the German maid's room, finds her mas-
turbating on the bed, buggers her, and tells her, 'You're a
Nazi.'

' "*Ja*." She shook her head. "No, no," she went on. "*Ja*,
don't stop. *Ja*." ' Later the maid says, ' "Mr. Rojack, I do not
know why you have trouble with your wife. You are absolutely a genius, Mr. Rojack." '

Cherry, Rojack's next love of the same long night, votes

the same sex ticket. A nightclub singer, ravished in the past by Bugsy Seigal, boxers, hoodlums, fabled Negro entertainers, and millionaires, says to Rojack, '. . . it happened with you. I had an orgasm with you. I was never able to before.'

Following *Advertisements* there came *Deaths For The Ladies* (*and other disasters*), a book of poems in which Mailer seemed to be making engaging fun of himself.

'   If
Harry Golden
is the gentile's
Jew
        can I be-
come the Golden
Goy?'

But he also appeared to be committing himself even more irretrievably to becoming another wowser on the scene, a personality, rather than a working writer. That is to say, I doubt that the poems ever would have been published had they not been written by a celebrity.

Then, only last year, along came *The Presidential Papers*, another compilation, with one redeeming stunning piece (on the Patterson–Liston fight) and rather more hard-sell advertisements. The book was written with 'the idea that the President might come to read it' but, on publication, Kennedy had already been assassinated. In the *Papers*, Mailer wrote,

'Jack Kennedy won the election by one hundred thousand votes. . . . So I came to the cool conclusion I had won the election for Kennedy with my piece in *Esquire* (Superman Comes to the Supermarket), the thought might be high presumption, but it was not unique. I had done something curious but indispensible for the campaign – succeeded in making it dramatic.'

Between books, Mailer had run for Mayor of New York and had been the subject of a piece in *Esquire* by James Baldwin. '. . . our styles are very different,' Baldwin wrote, 'I am a black boy from the Harlem streets, and Norman is a middle-class Jew . . . I hope I do not need to say no sneer is implied in the above description of Norman.' He continued, '. . . Negro musicians . . . who really liked Norman did not for an instant consider him as being even remotely "hip". . . . They thought he was a real sweet ofay cat, but a little frantic.' Baldwin suggested that the trouble between Mailer and himself was 'the toughest kid on the block meeting the toughest kid on the block.'

The rumble did not end there. Soon the Original Original Toughest Kid On The Block was heard from: Nelson Algren. In *Who Lost An American*, he wrote, 'A fellow wearing a sandwich-board advertising himself approached me. "I am Norman Manlifellow," he introduced himself, sheathing a nine-inch jacknife, "Hemingway never wrote anything that would disturb an eight-year-old." ' And still later. ' "I'm a writer, *not* a performer," he (Manlifellow) explained . . . and thereupon stood on his head; revealing, as his trousers slipped to his knees, that one of his socks bore the legend, "Look at me!" and the other the plea, "*Keep* Looking!" '

While the toughest kids on the block were brawling under an *Esquire* street lamp, the men were sitting inside writing novels. Like *Herzog*.

And now Mailer has published his first novel in nine years, *An American Dream*. 'He wrote it at high pitch,' according to the blurb, 'each chapter appearing in *Esquire*, while he was still at work on the next: a method now unusual but common enough among the great novelists of the nineteenth century, which contributed much to the quivering tension of the story.' The novel got off to a bad critical start. On Sunday, April 25,

John Coleman wrote in the *Observer*, '. . . it's appallingly awful, bad and embarrassing in self-indulgent ways one isn't used to seeing out there in print.' Cyril Connolly was more magnanimous in the *Sunday Times*. He found the first few pages 'superbly written', but 'about page 165 the rot sets in and from 200 to the end I found the going difficult. One can sum up that he proves himself a novelist even if he hasn't written a very good novel. He must try again.'

Six o'clock the same evening Mailer spoke at the Mayfair Theatre. Once more you had to admire his courage, but regret his recklessness. There were more than 300 people in the theatre, an audience that included critics, other novelists, editors, and playwrights. Sympathizers. 'A frightfully hip audience,' the insufferably smart John Crosby wrote in the *Herald-Tribune*, 'that included people like Jonathan Miller, Ken Tynan, bevies of beautiful girls with long blonde hair, carefully ironed in the latest fashion. A sprinkling of Negros, and all three sexes.' The *Sun* ran a story under the headline HOW CAN THESE PEOPLE BE SO STUPID? The report described Mailer as 'A fleshy Chico Marx' and quoted the chairman, Malcolm Muggeridge, as saying Mailer was 'a moralist with this intense loathing that all decent people must feel for the Twentieth Century,' adding its own comment. 'Right. And there is no aspect of the Twentieth Century that should attract more intense loathing than a bunch of highly articulate, talented, sensitive, intelligent people exhibiting such crass stupidity in public. And gloating at their wisdom.' The *Evening Standard*, on the other hand, felt it was an 'excellent entertainment. . . . Anyone looking for a wild advocate of violence was certainly disappointed. Endearing is not an unfair description.' But the most tender account was written by Terry Coleman for the *Guardian*. 'He has a presence,' he wrote. 'He is a sympathetic man.' But Coleman felt *An American Dream* was nasty, brutish, and long.

'How can he do this? How can he talk like a Puritan, so evidently concerned, and then write like Hank Janson? He can write so strongly and well. "The Deer Park" so much abused, is a fine novel: the sympathy between his characters is plain, and between his characters and himself. But it seems "The Deer Park" is not Hollywood any longer. It isn't Mailer, either.'

Mailer began by promising us a definition of existentialism, which he never quite got around to. He spoke with regret for the eighteenth century when society was orderly and the British navy and the orgasm were both going good; and then he remembered to put in a word for the folks in Alaska who live in a heroic relation to nature. He was, like most of us, against the piggish rich and for an end to the war in Vietnam. He made some perceptive remarks about the split personality of minority group men – their image of themselves against society's image of them. He complained about the shrinking purchase power of the pound and the decline of craftsmanship, ugly architecture, greedy doctors, and high taxation, sounding uncannily like J. B. Priestley in one of those *Notes From The Wilderness* he used to write for the *New Statesman*.

It was inchoate, but charming, for Mailer is certainly an engaging man. When he smiles his whole face rumples; it is suffused by the most infectious warmth. Then pulling at his ear lobe, making a fist, discovering it with something like admiration, he told us that we were living through a sexual revolution. Sex, once so ring-a-ding, had been corrupted by the search for status, and now Mailer felt that all the cool cats in the house had to be brave in bed. He also seemed to think that promiscuity was a malaise peculiar to the twentieth century.

By this time I held Mailer in a double-vision. I could hear the self-inflated, innocent programmist going on and on about a sexual revolution, but what I saw was a warm chunky man of forty-two who was really saying that screwing today wasn't nearly as satisfying as when he was a kid and that, like the rest of us, he suffered sourness and insults in and out of bed, and wasn't it a shame, a bloody shame.

Afterwards, outside the Mayfair Hotel, it seemed that nearly everybody was making condescending jokes, shaking their heads, and feeling sorry for Mailer. I can remember being angry because at first there was a sort of ugly self-satisfaction that I felt and sensed in others around me. There goes Mailer, rich and famous, unlike you and I, but what a goddamn fool. Then I recall feeling let down because it was just this kind of exhibition which gave licence to modish newspaper columnists to poke fun at a man who has, remember, written outstandingly well on occasion.

It was similar to the disappointment one felt after seeing *The World Of Paul Slickey*, *John Osborne's* wild attack on Fleet Street gossip columnists, so inaccurate and badly conceived as to ultimately give pleasure to its odious target. It was why, on balance, *Not So Much A Programme* was that infuriating. Most of the attacks mounted were so loaded and juvenile as to fortify institutions and personalities we had hitherto abhorred.

And what, then, of *An American Dream* itself? If the man we saw on stage at the Mayfair Theatre was 'mild Clark Kent' then this *alter ego*, *Superman*, flies in the fiction. Steve Rojack, like Sergius O'Shaugnessy before him, is a man of stunning accomplishments. 'The one intellectual in America's history with a D.S.C.' He is a former congressman, a TV personality, and the author of "The Psychology of the Hangman". In an opening calculated to stop you from switching channels, Rojack informs the reader, 'I met Jack Kennedy in November, 1946. We were both war heroes, and had just been elected to Congress.'

The story, told in the first person, begins with Rojack

murdering his rich bitch wife after a quarrel. Then he buggers the German maid and throws his wife's body out on to the street. At the police station, Rojack outmanoeuvres the cops; he meets a Mafia gangster and Cherry, a gorgeous nightclub singer. Rojack and Cherry make love only after he has proven he has *cojones* by standing up to some thugs in the nightclub. Then Rojack out-talks the cops again and puts down Shago Martin (a famous Negro entertainer and Cherry's previous lover) and makes love to Cherry again. Finally, Rojack comes face to face with Oswald Kelly, his dead wife's step-father and something of a Daddy Warbucks figure. For Kelly's sake, Rojack walks a wind-swept parapet thirty storeys above Manhattan. Cherry dies. Rojack goes to Las Vegas, picks up more than twenty-four thousand dollars at the dice tables, stops at a phone booth and rings Cherry in heaven. '. . . the girls are swell,' Cherry says. 'Marilyn says to say hello.'

This is not so much fiction as a comic strip fantasy. Rojack not only deals out first orgasms to lucky girls, but is congratulated on his manhood wherever he wanders. The cops end up admiring him, Shago Martin tells him he has *valour*, and you feel that even Kelly wants to hug him. While Rojack is with Kelly, the phone rings. ' "It was Jack," he said to me. "He said to send you his regards and commiserations . . . I didn't know you knew him," ' Rojack's wife, it turns out, was a CIA agent. So, possibly, is Ruta. Maybe Cherry too.

An American Dream, as John Coleman, Christopher Ricks, and Al Alvarez have already written, is a big bad novel, a novel so obviously appalling, that after reading what they had to say I re-read the book, hoping to find a hidden vein of genius somewhere. If it's there, it eluded me. The one outstanding virtue of *An American Dream* is a solid old-fashioned one. Mailer, though he now has a weakness for windy passages, still has an astonishing narrative skill. When he wants to tell a story he tells it very well, indeed. The scenes in the police station are first-rate.

Or have we all missed the point and is *An American Dream* meant to be a comic strip extension of reality? The first pop novel? If so, it's still sub-standard.

In *Advertisements For Myself* Mailer wrote, '. . . for years he (Hemingway) has not written anything which would bother an eight-year-old or one's grandmother. . . . Hemingway has always been afraid to think, afraid of losing even a little popularity, and so today he clowns away his time worrying publicly about the feud between his good friends Leonard Lyons and Walter Winchell, and his words excite no thought in the best of my rebel generation. He's no longer any help to us, he's left us marooned in the nervous boredom of a world which finally he didn't try hard enough to change.'

It's still too early to write off Norman Mailer. One still hopes he will stop clowning and settle down to the book he has talked about for so many years. But if he does have a perception that will settle for nothing less than making a revolution in the consciousness of our time then the sour truth is he is still imprisoned with it.

These days it's not very risky to be a Jew. It is, however, becoming increasingly tricky to make out as an American-Jewish novelist and be original as well, the overriding fear being that everything has been said. The claustrophobic (eat, boychick, eat) tenement background most of us escaped from in one city or another has been caught exactly by Henry Roth, Daniel Fuchs (in a masterful trilogy) and more recently, Alfred Kazin. Such protest as we had in us was scorchingly made by Jerome Weidman, Budd Shulberg and Irwin Shaw, all lately given to big flatulent novels. In an astonishingly short time there has been a sweeping cultural change. Our fathers struggled to educate us, we compete, leading with the elbows, for foundation grants. The campus in the cornfields has displaced the garment district (I Can Get It For You Wholesale) and then Hollywood (What Makes Sammy Run, The Day Of The Locust) as the canvas for Jewish fiction. The archetypal ineffectual hero in today's Jewish-American novel holds tenure at a mid-Western university, usually the pillowy creative writing chair where Herzog, Gabriel Wallach (Philip Roth's *Letting Go*) and Seymour Levin (Malamud's *A New Life*) are already toiling, marking mss between pot-parties and committing insults and shiksas to memory for novels-in-progress. Nobody is more aware of the humour inherent in the Jewish cultural takeover than the spoilers themselves, as witness Wallace Markfield's hilarious send-up of Jewish intellectual life in *To An Early Grave* or Leslie Fiedler's professor, Baro Finklestone, in *Back to China*, who observes, 'one controversial Jew from the East was really all so small and remote a Western university could bear.'

Such in fact is the choked traffic in novels about wisecracking, soul-searching, sobbing urban Jews, that recently one of the most imaginative of them, Bruce Jay Friedman's *Stern*, was largely overlooked in England, consigned to everybody's bottom of the novel column ('Another funny Jewish-American. . . .')

The file on Jewish-American experiences seems complete in *An American Dream*. Norman Mailer even coloured in the horror comic fantasy, screwing the German maid for a generation of affluent but guilt-ridden Jews. In *Herzog*, which was acclaimed everywhere and won the American National Book Award, Saul Bellow triumphantly trapped us into accepting that Fucky-Knuckles and cuckold Moses E. Herzog, Ph.D., as a hero of our times.

Undoubtedly, recent Jewish-American novelists have over-reached each other in greedily assuming guilt for all the world's ills, making it intellectually fashionable (but boring and presumptuous) to argue that if contemporary man is alienated, no one is more alienated than the Jew. Then along came Leslie Fiedler with *Back To China*, wherein he typically outgrabbed everyone else, threatening to run the Jewish comic novel right off the tracks and into the ravine. His in-effectual Jewish professor, Baro Finklestone, feels so guilty about Hiroshima that he has a Japanese doctor punish him by performing a vasectomy on him. To ask more, it seemed to me at the time, would be sadistic.

With the exception of Mailer, Joseph Heller and now possibly Bellow, I suspect the Jewish-American novel is much more widely written about than read in England, the mis-taken assumption being that they are all the same. Jewish therefore funny just as some ill-informed Americans would have it that Amis and Braine or Penelope Mortimer and Edna O'Brien are interchangeable, being British therefore swinging.

The best of the Jewish-American novelists speak in accents distinctly their own, they differ widely in approach, but most of them do share certain characteristics. They find the aspiring Jewish middle class ugly or, at best, a target for excoriating satire, and they are inclined to look back on the days of tenement poverty with nostalgia. Many of these same novelists, so recently assimilated and become an integral part of American culture, tend to feel displaced. A case in point was Herzog's touching need to attach himself to the land, in his case, the Berkshires. If Jewish-American writers have escaped the ghetto they have, to their credit, never quite put it behind them, and recently they seem to have begun to worry more and more about their origins. On a coarse, show-biz level this has given us the indecently sentimental *Fiddler On The Roof* (ha ha, it's a pogrom) and a number of Thirties protest novels redone as zippy musicals. More seriously, Norman Mailer has recently written commentaries on Martin Buber's *Tales of the Hasidim* for *Commentary*, and now Malamud has come forth with a novel set in Russia, reaching back to the *shtetl*, the Pale of Settlement, and the time of Tsar Nicolas II: a period we more readily associate with Isaac Babel and Isaac Bashevis Singer.

'One thinks a good deal about the subject matter of his fiction,' Malamud said, accepting the National Book Award for *The Fixer*, and then he went on to quote Melville, 'To produce a mighty book you must choose a mighty theme,' though he allowed he was not sure about the corollary, that one couldn't write a great and enduring work about the life of a flea.

The mighty theme Bernard Malamud has chosen for himself is the resistance of a meek Jew to the charge of ritual murder, in short a novel inspired by the infamous trial of Mendel Beiliss, a clerk in Kiev, who was arrested for the ritual murder of a Christian boy in 1913, a time when crazed anti-Semitism was rampant in Russia, following the disastrous war with Japan coupled with the demand for liberal reforms; a period when *The Protocols of the Elders of Zion* were being widely devoured and the Tsar himself wore a Black Hundreds button on his lapel.

The Union of the Russian People, or more popularly the Black Hundreds, Norman Cohn writes, in his first-rate *Warrant For Genocide*, marked 'an important stage in the transition from reactionary politics as they were understood in the 19th century to the right-wing totalitarianism of the Nazis. . . . Like the Nazis, (the Black Hundreds) pretended that the Jews formed a capitalist-revolutionary conspiracy, and that in order to prevent this conspiratorial body from establishing a monstrous tyranny, the workers and peasants must stand firmly by their "native" ruling class.'

The Fixer, Yakov Bok, is, to begin with, a pathetic figure, the quintessential Jewish loser, orphaned by a pogrom and abandoned by his wife after their marriage has failed to produce a child. At the age of 31, dizzy with Spinoza (as was Asa Heshel in I. B. Singer's *The Family Moskat*), he shaves off his beard and moves out of the *shtetl*, the Hasidic village, to Kiev, in search of a better life and hopefully a stake to take him to America. In Kiev, he rescues a drunken merchant – Maximovitch, who wears a Black Hundreds button – from certain death in the snow and, concealing his own Jewishness from him, is rewarded first with a plastering and painting job and finally with the position of overseer of Maximovitch's brickworks, which obliges Bok to live in a district forbidden to Jews. In his new job, Bok immediately antagonizes the workers, cutting down on their stealing. He drives the schoolboys who pelt him with stones off the lot. One night he rescues a wandering old Jew from anti-Semitic ruffians and hides him in his room over the stables. A few days later, shortly before Easter, a notorious time for pogroms, one of the schoolboys is found stabbed to death in a cave, the blood drained from his body. Bok is arrested, revealed as a Jew, and charged with ritual murder, an accusation first brought against the Jews in the 12th century, the unspeakable lie being that Jews required blood for the making of Passover matzohs.

For the rest, Yakov Bok is imprisoned, lingering in a cell for two years awaiting trial. Bok's one possible ally, the decent examining magistrate, who instantly sees that he is innocent, is imprisoned himself and hanged in his cell. The other officials, fanatic anti-semites, proceed to frame Bok monstrously and, determined to squeeze a confession from him, heap indignity upon indignity. On the advice of a priest, an 'expert' on Jewish matters, the officials watch Bok in his cell, infuriated when his menstrual period fails to begin. Bok is stripped naked and searched six times daily. He is put in irons. He is offered free passage out of Russia if only he will sign a confession. If he doesn't sign, if he is acquitted, he is told he will be responsible for a pogrom, for his crime is now widely known and the people are aroused against him. It is Yakov Bok's triumph, that grown strong and morally conscious through suffering, he refuses to sign a confession and, in the end, he is led off to his trial. To be found guilty, we assume, for the evidence has been faked. The Tsar himself has expressed interest, and the judge is a carefully picked anti-Semite.

> ' "Why me?" Bok asks himself, a poor, half-ignorant fixer? Once you leave you're out in the open; it rains and it snows. It snows history, which means what happens to somebody starts in a web of events outside the personal. It starts of course before we get there. We're all in history, that's sure, but some are more than others. Jews more than some. If it snows not everybody is out in it getting wet. He had been doused.'

There is much to admire in *The Fixer*, many of Bernard Malamud's rare virtues as a writer being much in evidence. The novel is rich in invention, surprisingly comic at times, seldom tract-like, always a pleasure to read in spite of the sickening subject matter. It is a worthy novel, maybe even a noble one, but in the end, unlike *The Assistant* or the splendid stories in *The Magic Barrel*, the novel is curiously without an inner life, a will of its own. *The Fixer*, it seems to me, is a novel forced in the humanist's greenhouse. As an evocation of the *shtetl*, of Jewish life in Tsarist Russia, it is not to be compared, for instance, with the stories of Isaac Babel or I. B. Singer, but with other intellectual acts of goodwill, fabricated novels, about the Jewish tragedy, say John Hersey's underrated *The Wall*.

It is a case, I fear, of a natural writer, but a highbrow, having turned his hand to a middlebrow form. *The Fixer* is expertly made. But its very virtues (racy, narrative, surprise chapter endings) coming from a writer of Malamud's stature, taste oddly sour.

In *The Fixer*, as in so many middlebrow novels or films, there is hardly an effect without an exact cause, the trouble being, given the cause, we quickly sense what's coming. When Yakov Bok, plastering the flat for the merchant Maximovitch, is pursued everywhere by his sex-starved daughter, finally rejecting her at the last minute when he discovers that she is unclean, menstruating, we immediately grasp that come his arrest, the insulted girl will charge him with sexual assault, and so she does. Then it is sad to see Malamud, a writer with an ear for all the nuances of dialogue, trapped, within the dubious framework of the historical novel, into stuffing people's mouths with awkward but necessary exposition-ridden talk. The lawyer Ostrofsky tells Yakov Bok,

> 'Your case is tied up with the frustrations of recent Russian history. The Russo-Japanese war, I don't have to tell you, was a terrible disaster, but it brought on the Revolution of 1905, which was coming anyway. . . . This was good for Russia but bad for the Jews. The

government, as usual, blamed us for their troubles and not one day after the Tsar's concessions pogroms started simultaneously in three hundred towns. Of course you know this, what Jew doesn't?'

I don't have to tell you. Of course you know this. Yes, but the reader doesn't.

When he accepted the National Book Award in New York last month, Malamud said, 'If one is, as an individual, moved by themes that could be called mighty, obviously it will pay to seek them out. . . .' Malamud has now done his duty by the 'mighty theme', and one hopes he will now return to chronicles of the 'fleas' of his time, a form in which he is most likely to leave us with an enduring work.

Any account of the Catskill Mountains must begin with Grossinger's. The G. On either side of the highway out of New York and into Sullivan County, a two hour drive north, one is assailed by billboards. DO A JERRY LEWIS – COME TO BROWN'S. CHANGE TO THE FLAGLER. I FOUND A HUSBAND AT THE WALDEMERE. THE RALEIGH IS ICIER, NICIER, AND SPICIER. All the Borscht Belt billboards are criss-crossed with lists of attractions, each hotel claiming the ultimate in golf courses, the latest indoor and outdoor pools, and the most tantalizing parade of stars. The countryside between the signs is ordinary, without charm. Bush land and small hills. And then finally one comes to the Grossinger billboard. All it says, *sotto voce*, is GROSSINGER'S HAS EVERYTHING.

'On a day in August, 1914, that was to take its place among the red-letter days of all history,' begins a booklet published to commemorate Grossinger's 50th anniversary, 'a war broke out in Europe. Its fires seared the world. . . . On a summer day of that same year, a small boarding house was opened in the Town of Liberty.' The farm house was opened by Selig and Malke Grossinger to take in nine people at nine dollars a week. Fresh air for factory workers, respite for tenement dwellers. Now Grossinger's, spread over a thousand acres, can accommodate fifteen hundred guests. It represents an investment of fifteen million dollars. But to crib once more from the anniversary booklet, 'The greatness of any institution cannot be measured by material size alone. The Taj Mahal cost a king's ransom but money in its intrinsic form is not a part of that structure's unequalled beauty.'

Grossinger's, on first sight, looks like the consummate kibbutz. Even in the absence of arabs there is a security guard at the gate. It has its own water supply, a main building

– in this case Sullivan County Tudor with picture windows – and a spill of outlying lodges named after immortals of the first Catskill Aliya, like Eddie Cantor and Milton Berle.

I checked in on a Friday afternoon in summer and crossing the terrace to my quarters stumbled on a Grossinger's Forum Of The Air in progress. Previous distinguished speakers – a reflection, as one magazine put it, of Jennie Grossinger, in whom the traditional reverence for learning remains undimmed – have included Max Lerner and Norman Cousins. This time out the lecturer was resident hypnotist Nat Fleischer, who was taking a stab at CAN LOVE SURVIVE MARRIAGE? 'I have a degree in psychology,' Fleischer told me, 'and am now working on my doctorate.'

'Where?'

'I'd rather not say.'

There were about a hundred and fifty potential hecklers on the terrace. All waiting to pounce. Cigar-chumpers in Bermuda shorts and ladies ready with an alternative of the New York *Post* on their laps. 'Men are past their peak at twenty-five,' Fleischer shouted into the microphone, 'but ladies reach theirs much later and stay on a plateau, *while the men are tobogganing downhill*.' One man hooted, another guffawed, but many ladies clapped approval. 'You think', Fleischer said, 'the love of the baby for his momma is natural – *no*!' A man, holding a silver foil sun reflector to his face, dozed off. The lady beside him fanned herself with *From Russia, With Love*. 'In order to remain sane,' Fleischer continued, 'what do we need? ALL OF US. Even at sixty and seventy. LOVE. A little bit of love. If you've been married for twenty-five years you shouldn't take your wife for granted. Be considerate.'

A lady under a tangle of curlers bounced up and said, 'I've been married twenty-*nine years* and my husband doesn't take me for granted.'

This alarmed a sunken-bellied man in the back row. He didn't join in the warm applause. Instead he stood up to peer at the lady. 'I'd like to meet her husband.' Sitting down again, he added, 'The *shmock*.'

There was to be a get-together for singles in the evening, but the prospects did not look dazzling. A truculent man sitting beside me in the bar said, 'I dunno. I swim this morning. I swim this afternoon – indoors, outdoors – my God, what a collection! When are all the beauties checking in?'

I decided to take a stroll before dinner. The five lobbies at Grossinger's are nicely panelled in pine, but the effect is somewhat undermined by the presence of plastic plants everywhere. There is plastic sweet corn for sale in the shop beside the Olympic-size outdoor pool and plastic grapes are available in the Mon Ami Gift and Sundry Shop in the main building. Among those whose pictures hang on The Wall Of Fame are Cardinal Spellman and Yogi Berra, Irving Berlin, Governors Harriman and Rockefeller, Ralph Bunche, Zero Mostel, and Herman Wouk. The indoor pool, stunningly simple in design, still smelled so strongly of disinfectants that I was reminded of the more modest 'Y' pool of my boyhood. I fled. Grossinger's has its own post office and is able to stamp all mail 'Grossinger, N.Y.' There is also Grossinger Lake, 'for your tranquil togetherness'; an 18-hole golf course; stables; an outdoor artificial ice rink; a ski trail and toboggan run; a His'n Hers health club; and of course a landing strip adjoining the hotel, the Jennie Grossinger Field.

The ladies had transformed themselves for dinner. Gone were the curlers, out came the minks. 'Jewish security blankets,' a guest, watching the parade with me, called the wraps, but fondly, with that sense of self-ridicule that redeems Grossinger's and, incidentally, makes it the most slippery of places to write about.

I suppose it would be easiest, and not unjustified, to present the Catskills as a cartoon. A Disneyland with knishes. After all, everywhere you turn the detail is bizarre. At the Concord, for instance, a long hall of picture windows overlooks a parking lot. There are rooms that come with two adjoining bathrooms. ('It's a gimmick. People like it. They talk about it.') All the leading hotels now have indoor ice skating rinks because, as the lady who runs The Laurels told me, our guests find it too cold to skate outside. True, they have not yet poured concrete into the natural lakes to build artificial filtered pools above, but, short of that, every new convenience conspires to protect guests from the countryside. Most large hotels, for instance, link outlying lodges to the main building through a system of glassed-in and sometimes even subterranean passages, all in the costly cause of protecting people from the not notoriously fierce Catskills outdoors.

What I'm getting at is that by a none too cunning process of selected detail one can make Grossinger's, the Catskills, and the people who go there, appear totally grotesque. One doesn't, because there's more to it than that. Nothing, on the other hand, can prevent Sullivan County from seeming outlandish, for outlandish it certainly is, and it would be condescending, the most suspect sort of liberalism, to overlook this and instead celebrate, say, Jennie Grossinger's maudlin 'warmth' or 'traditional reverence' for bogus learning.

Something else. The archetypal Grossinger's guest belongs to the most frequently fired at class of American Jews. Even as *Commentary* sends out another patrol of short story writers the *Partisan Review* irregulars are waiting in the bushes, bayonets drawn. Saul Bellow is watching, Alfred Kazin is ruminating, Norman Mailer is ready with his flick-knife, and who knows what manner of trip wires the next generation of Jewish writers is laying out at this very moment. Was there ever a group so pursued by such an unsentimental platoon of chroniclers? So plagued by moralists? So blamed for making money? Before them came the *luftmensh*, the impecunious dreamers – tailors, cutters, corner grocers – so adored by Bernard Malamud. After them came Phillip Roth's confident college boys on the trot, Americans who just happen to have had a Jewish upbringing. But this generation be-tween, this unlovely spiky bunch that climbed with the rest of middle-class America out of the depression into a pot of prosperity, is the least liked by literary Jews. In a Clifford Odets play they were the rotters. The rent-collectors. Next Jerome Weidman carved them up and then along came Budd Schulberg and Irwin Shaw. In fact in all this time only Herman Wouk, armed with but a slingshot of clichés, has come to their defence. More of an embarrassment, I'd say, than a shield.

Well now here they are at Grossinger's, sitting ducks for satire. Manna for sociologists. Here they are, breathless, but at play, so to speak, suffering sour stomach and cancer scares, one Israeli bond drive after another, unmarriageable daugh-ters and sons gone off to help the Negroes overcome in Mississippi. Grossinger's is their dream of plenty realized, but if you find it funny, larger than life, then so do the regu-lars. In fact there is no deflating remark I could make about minks or match-making that has not already been made by visiting comedians or guests. Furthermore, for an innocent goy to even think some of the things said at Grossinger's would be to invite the wrath of the B'nai Brith Anti-Defamation League.

At Grossinger's, guests are offered the traditional foods, but in super-abundance, which may not have been the case for many of them in the early years. Here, too, are the big TV comics, only this is their real audience and they appreciate it. They reveal the authentic joke behind the bland story they had to tell on TV because Yiddish punch-lines do not make for happy Neilson ratings.

The 'ole swimmin' hole', as one Catskill ad says, was never like this. Or to quote from an ad for Kutsher's Country Club, 'You wouldn't have liked The Garden of Eden anyway – it didn't have a golf course. Kutsher's, on the other hand. . . .' There are all the knishes a man can eat and, at Brown's

Hotel, they are made more palatable by being called 'Roulade of Fresh Chicken Livers'. In the same spirit, the familiar chicken soup with *lockshen* has been reborn 'essence of chicken broth with fine noodles' on yet another menu.

The food at Grossinger's, the best I ate in the Catskills, is delicious if you like traditional kosher cooking. But entering the vast dining-room, which seats some 1600 guests, creates an agonizing moment for singles. 'The older men want young girls,' David Geivel, the head waiter told me, 'and the girls want presentable men. They want to line up a date for New York where they sit alone all week. They've only got two days, you know, so they've got to make it fast. After each meal they're always wanting to switch tables. The standard complaint from the men runs . . . "even when the girls are talking to me, they're looking over my shoulder to the dentist at the next table. Why should I ask her for a date, such an eye-roamer?" '

I picked up a copy of the daily *Tattler* at my table and saw how, given one bewitching trip through the hotel Gestetner, the painfully shy old maid and the flat-chested girl and the good-natured lump were transformed into 'sparkling, captivating' Barbara, Ida, 'the fun-loving frolicker'; and Miriam, 'a charmladen lass who makes a visit to table 20F a must'. I also noted that among other 'typewriter boys' who had stayed at 'the G.' there was Paddy Chayefsky and Paul Gallico. Dore Schary was a former editor of the *Tattler* and Shelley Winters, Betty Garrett, and Robert Alda had all once worked on the special staff. Students from all over the United States still compete for jobs at the hotel. They can clear as much as a hundred and fifty dollars a week and, as they say at the G., be nice to your bus boy, next year when he graduates he may treat your ulcer. My companions at the table included two forlorn bachelors, a teenager with a flirtatious aunt, and a bejewelled and wizened widow in her sixties. 'I hate to waste all this food,' the widow said, 'it's such a crime. My dog should be here he'd have a wonderful time.'

'Where is he?'

'Dead,' she said, false eyelashes fluttering, just as the loudspeaker crackled and the get-together for singles was announced. 'Single people *only*, please.'

The teenager turned on her aunt. 'Are you going to dance with Ray again?'

'Why not? He's excellent.'

'Sure, sure. Only he's a *faigele*.' A homosexual.

'Did you see the girl in the Mexican squaw blanket? She told her mother, "I'm going to the singles. If I don't come back to the room tonight you'll know I'm engaged." What an optimist!'

The singles get-together was thinly attended. A disaster. Bachelors looked in, muttered, pulled faces, and departed in pairs. The ladies in their finery were abandoned in the vast ballroom to the flatteries of staff members, twisting in turn with the hairdresser and the dance teacher, each of whom had an eye for tomorrow's trade. My truculent friend of the afternoon had resumed his station at the bar. 'Hey,' he said, turning on a 'G-man' (a staff member), 'where'd you get all those dogs? You got a contract with New York City maybe they send you all the losers?'

The G-man, his manner reverent, told me that this bar was the very place where Eddie Cantor had discovered Eddie Fisher, who was then just another unknown singing with the band. 'If you had told me in those days that Fisher would get within even ten feet of Elizabeth Taylor –' He stopped short, overcome. 'The rest', he said, 'is history.'

Ladies began to file into the Terrace Room, the husbands trailing after them with the mink stoles now slung nonchalantly over their arms. Another All-Star Friday Nite Revue had finished in the Playhouse.

'What was it like?' somebody asked.

'Aw. It goes with the *gefilte* fish.'

Now the spotlight was turned on the Prentice Minner Four. Minner, a talented and militant Negro, began with a rousing civil liberties song. He sang, 'From San Francisco to New York Island, this is your land and mine.'

'Do you know Shadrach?' somebody called out.

'Old Man River?'

'What about Tzena Tzena?'

Minner compromised. He sang Tzena Tzena, a hora, but with new lyrics. CORE lyrics.

A G-man went over to talk to my truculent friend at the bar. 'You can't sit down at a table,' he said, 'and say to a lady you've just met that she's, um, well-stacked. It's not refined.' He was told he would have to change his table again.

'Allright. O.K. I like women. So that makes me a louse.'

I retired early, with my G. fact sheets. More than 700,000 gallons of water, I read, are required to fill the outdoor pool. G. dancing masters, Tony and Lucille, introduced the mambo to this country. Henry Cabot Lodge has, as they say, graced the G. roster. So has Robert Kennedy. Others I might have rubbed shoulders with are Baron Edmund de Rothschild and Rocky Marciano. It was Damon Runyon who first called Grossinger's 'Lindy's with trees'. Nine world boxing champions have trained for title bouts at the hotel. Barney Ross, who was surely the first orthodox Jew to become lightweight champion, 'scrupulously abjured the general frolicsome air that pervaded his camp' in 1934. Not so goy-boy, Ingemar Johansson, the last champ to train at Grossinger's.

In the morning I decided to forgo the recommended early riser's appetizer, a baked Idaho potato; I also passed up herring baked and fried, waffles and watermelon, blueberries, strawberries, bagels and lox, and French toast. I settled for orange juice and coffee and slipped outside for a fast cigarette. (Smoking is forbidden on the sabbath, from sunset Friday to sundown Saturday, in the dining-room and the main lobbies.) Lou Goldstein, Director of Daytime Social Activities, was running his famous game of Simon Says on the terrace. There were at least a hundred eager players and twice as many hecklers. 'Simon says put up your hands. Simon says bend forward from the waist. The *waist*, lady. You got one? oi. *That's* bending? What's your name?'

'Mn Mn,' through buttoned lips.

'Allright. Simon says what's your name?'

'Sylvia.'

'Now that's a good Jewish name. The names they have these days. Désirée. Drexel. Where are you from?'

'Philadelphia.'

'*Out.*'

A man cupped his hands to his mouth and called out, 'Tell us the one about the two *goyim*.'

'We don't use that word here. There are people of every faith at Grossinger's. In fact, we get all kinds here. (Allright, lady. Sit down. We saw the outfit.) Last year a lady stands here and I say to her what do you think of sex. Sex, she says, it's a fine department store.' Goldstein announced a horse shoe toss for the men, but there were no takers. 'Listen here,' he said, 'at Grossinger's you don't work. You toss the horse shoe but a member of our staff picks it up. Also you throw downhill. Allright, athletes, follow me.'

I stayed behind for a demonstration on how to apply make-up. A volunteer was called for, a plump matron stepped forward, and was helped on to a make-shift platform by the beautician. 'Now,' he began, 'I know that some of you are worried about the expression lines round your mouth. Well, this putty if applied correctly will fill all the crevices. . . . There, notice the difference on the right side of the lady's face?'

'No.'

'*I'm sure* the ladies in the first four rows can notice.'

Grossinger's has everything – and a myth. The myth of

Jennie, LIVING SYMBOL 'HOTEL WITH A HEART' runs a typical *Grossinger News* headline. There are photographs everywhere of Jennie with celebrities. 'A local landmark', says a Grossinger's brochure, 'is the famous smile of the beloved Jennie.' A romantic but mediocre oil painting of Jennie hangs in the main lobby. There has been a song called *Jennie* and she has appeared on *This Is Your Life*, an occasion so thrilling that as a special treat on rainy days guests are sometimes allowed to watch a rerun of the tape. But Jennie, now in her seventies, can no longer personally bless all the honeymoon couples who come to the hotel. Neither can she 'drift serenely' through the vast dining-room as often as she used to, and so a younger lady, Mrs. Sylvia Jacobs, now fills many of Jennie's offices. Mrs. Jacobs, in charge of Guest Relations, is seldom caught without a smile. 'Jennie', she told me, 'loves all human beings, regardless of race, colour, or creed. Nobody else has her vision and charm. She personifies the grace and dignity of a great lady.'

Jennie herself picked Mrs. Jacobs to succeed her as hostess at the G.

'God, I think, gives people certain gifts – God-given things like a voice,' Mrs. Jacobs said. 'Well, I was born into this business. In fifty years I am the one who comes closest to personifying the vision of Jennie Grossinger. The proof of the pudding is my identification here.' Just in case further proof was required, Mrs. Jacobs showed me letters from guests, tributes to her matchmaking and joy-spreading powers. You are, one letter testified, T-E-R-R-I-F-I-C. You have an atomic personality. 'There's tradition,' she said, 'and natural beauty and panoramic views in abundance here. We don't need Milton Berle. At Grossinger's, a seventy-five dollar a week stenographer can rub shoulders with a millionaire. This is an important facet of our activities, you know.'

'Do you deal with many complaints?' I asked.

Mrs. Jacobs melted me with a smile. 'A complaint isn't a

problem – it's a challenge. I thank people for their complaints.'

Mrs. Jacobs took me on a tour of Jennie's house, Joy Cottage, which is next door to Millionaire's Cottage and across the road from Pop's Cottage. A signed photograph of Chaim Weizmann, first president of Israel, rested on the piano, and a photograph of Jack Benny, also autographed, stood on the table alongside. One wall was covered from ceiling to floor with plaques. Inter-faith awards and woman-of-the-year citations, including The Noble Woman of the Year Award from the Baltimore Noble Ladies' Aid Society. There was also a Certificate of Honour from *Wisdom* magazine. 'Jennie', Mrs. Jacobs said, 'is such a modest woman. She is always studying, an hour a day, and if she meets a woman with a degree she is simply overcome. . . .' Jennie has only one degree of her own. An Honorary Doctor of Humanities awarded to her by Wilberforce University, Ohio, in 1959. 'I've never seen Jennie so moved', Mrs. Jacobs said, 'as when she was awarded that degree.'

Mrs. Jacobs offered me a box of cookies to sustain me for my fifteen minute drive to 'over there' – *dorten*, as they say in Yiddish – the Concord.

If Jennie Grossinger is the Dr. Schweitzer of the Catskills then Arthur Winarick must be counted its Dr. Strangelove. Winarick, once a barber, made his fortune with Jeris Hair Tonic, acquired the Concord for $10,000 in 1935, and is still, as they say, its guiding genius. He is in his seventies. On first meeting I was foolish enough to ask him if he had ever been to any of Europe's luxury resorts. 'Garages with drapes,' he said. 'Warehouses.'

A guest intruded; he wore a baseball cap with sunglasses fastened to the peak. 'What's the matter, Winarick, you only put up one new building this year?'

'*Three.*'

One of them is that 'exciting new sno-time rendezvous,'

King Arthur's Court, 'where every boy is a Galahad or a Lancelot and every damsel a Guinevere or a fair Elaine'. Winarick, an obsessive builder, once asked comedian Zero Mostel, 'What else can I do? What more can I add?'

'An indoor jungle, Arthur. Hunting for tigers under glass. On *shabus* the hunters could wear *yarmulkas*.' Skullcaps.

It is unlikely, however, that anyone at the Concord would ever wear a skullcap, for to drive from the G. to *dorten* is to leap a Jewish generation; it is to quit a *haimeshe* (homey) place, however schmaltzy, for chrome and concrete. The sweet but professional people-lovers of one hotel yield to the computer-like efficiency of another. The Concord, for instance, also has a problem with singles, but I would guess that there is less table-changing. Singles and marrieds, youngs and olds, are identified by different coloured pins plugged into a war plan of the dining-room.

The Concord is the largest and most opulent of the Catskill resorts. 'Today,' Walter Winchell recently wrote, 'it does 30 million Bux a year.' It's a fantastic place. A luxury liner permanently in dry dock. Nine storeys high with an enormous lobby, a sweep of red-carpeted stairway, and endless corridors leading here, there, and everywhere, the Concord can cope with 2,500 guests who can, I'm assured, consume 9,000 *latkas* and ten tons of meat a day. Ornate chandeliers drip from the ceiling of the main lobby. The largest of the hotel's three nightclubs, the Imperial Room, seats 2,500 people. But it is dangerous to attempt a physical description of the hotel. For even as I checked in, the main dining-room was making way for a still larger one, and it is just possible that since I left, the five inter-connecting convention halls have been opened up and converted into an indoor spring training camp for the Mets. Nothing's impossible. 'Years ago,' a staff member told me, 'a guest told Winarick you call this a room, at home I have a toilet nicer than such a room. And Winarick saw that he was right and began to build. "We're going to give them city living in the country," he said. Look at it this way. Everybody has the sun. Where do we go from there?'

Where they went was to build three golf courses, the last with 18 holes; hire five orchestras and initiate a big-name night-club policy (Milton Berle, Sammy Davis Jr., Judy Garland, Jimmy Durante, etc.); install a resident graphologist in one lobby ('Larry Hilton needs no introduction for his humorous Chalktalks. . . .') and a security officer, with revolver and bullet belt, to sit tall on his air-cushion before the barred vault in another; hire the most in life guards, Director of Water Activities, Buster Crabbe ('This magnificent outdoor pool', Crabbe recently wrote, 'makes all other pools look like the swimming hole I used to take Jane and the chimps to. . . .'); buy a machine, *the first in the Catskills*, to spew artificial and multi-coloured snow on the ski runs ('We had to cut out the coloured stuff, some people were allergic to it.'); and construct a shopping arcade, known as Little Fifth Avenue, in the lower lobby.

Mac Kinsbrunner, the genial resident manager, took me on a tour beginning with the shopping arcade. A sign read:

SHOW YOUR TALENT
Everyone's Doing It
PAINT A PICTURE YOURSELF
The Spin Art Shop
50 cents
5 x 7 oil painting
Only Non Allergic Paints Used

Next door, Tony and Marcia promised you could walk in and dance out doing the twist or the bossanova or pachanga or cha-cha.

'We've got five million bucks worth of stuff under construction here right now. People don't come to the mountains for a rest any more,' Kinsbrunner said, 'they want *tummel*.'

Tummel in Yiddish means noise and the old-time non-stop

Catskill comics were known as *tummlers* or noise-makers.

'In the old days, you know, we used to go in for callisthenics, but no more. People are older. Golf, O.K., but – well I'll tell you something – in these hotels we cater to what I call food-cholics. Anyway I used to run it – the callisthenics – one day I'm illustrating the pump, the bicycle pump exercise for fat people – you know, in-out, in-out – zoom – her guts come spilling out. A fat lady. Right out. There went one year's profits, no more callisthenics.'

We went to take a look at the health club. THRU THESE PORTALS, a sign read, Pass The Cleanest People In The World. 'I had that put up,' Kinsbrunner said. 'I used to be a school teacher.'

Another sign read:

FENCE FOR FUN

Mons. Octave Ponchez

Develop Poise – Grace – Physical Fitness

In the club for singles, Kinsbrunner said, 'Sure they're trouble. If a single doesn't hook up here she goes back to New York and says the food was bad. She doesn't say she's a dog. Me, I always tell them you should have been here last weekend. Boy.'

The Concord, indeed most of the Catskill resorts, now do a considerable out-of-season convention business. While I was staying at the hotel a group of insurance agents and their wives, coming from just about every state in the union, was whooping it up. *Their* theme-sign read:

ALL THAT GLITTERS

IS NOT GOLD

EXCEPT ANNUITIES

Groups representing different sales areas got into gay costumes to march into the dining-room for dinner. The men wore cardboard moustaches and Panama hats at rakish angles, and their wives wiggled shyly in hula skirts. Once inside the dining-room they all rose to sing a punchy sales song to the tune of 'Mac the Knife', from *The Threepenny Opera* by Bertold Brecht and Kurt Weill. It began, 'We're behind you/Old Jack Regan/To make Mutual number one. . . .' Then they bowed their heads in prayer for the company and held up lit sparklers for the singing of the national anthem.

The Concord is surrounded by a wire fence. It employs some thirty security men. But Mac Kinsbrunner, for one, is in favour of allowing outsiders to stroll through the hotel on Sundays. 'Lots of them', he told me 'can't afford the Concord yet. People come up in the world they want to show it, you know. They want other people to know they can afford it here. So let them come and look. It gives them something to work toward, something to look up to.'

The Concord must loom tallest from any one of a thousand *kochaleins* (literally 'cook-alones') and bungalow colonies that still operate in Sullivan County. Like Itzik's Rooms or the Bon-Repos or Altman's Cottages. Altman's is run by Ephraim Weisse, a most engaging man, a refugee, who has survived four concentration camps. 'The air is the only thing that's good in the Catskills,' Ephraim said. 'Business? It's murder. I need this bungalow colony like I need a hole in the head.' He shrugged, grinning. 'I survived Hitler, I'll outlast the Catskills.'

Other large hotels, not as celebrated as Grossinger's or the Concord, tend to specialize. The Raleigh, for instance, has five bands and goes in for young couples. LIVE 'LA DOLCE VITA' (the sweet life), the ads run, AT THE RALEIGH. 'We got the young swingers here,' the proprietor told me.

Brown's, another opulent place, is more of a family hotel. Jerry Lewis was once on their social staff and he still figures in most of their advertisements. Brown's is very publicity-conscious. Instead of playing Simon Says or the Concord variation, Simon Sez, they play Brown's Says. In fact as I entered the hotel lobby a member of the social staff was entertaining a group of ladies. 'The name of the game', he called out, 'is not bingo. It's BROWN'S. You win you yell out BROWN'S.'

Mrs. Brown told me that many distinguished people had stayed at her hotel. 'Among them, Jayne Mansfield and Mr. Haggerty.' Bernie Miller, *tummler*-in-residence, took me to see the hotel's pride, The Jerry Lewis Theatre-Club. 'Lots of big stars were embryos here,' he said.

Of all the hotels I visited in the Catskills only The Laurels does not serve kosher food and is actually built on a lake. Sackett Lake. But, oddly enough, neither the dining-room nor the most expensive bedrooms overlook the lake, and, as at the other leading resorts, there are pools inside and out, a skating rink, a health club, and a nightclub or two. 'People won't make their own fun any more,' said Arlene Damen, the young lady who runs the hotel with her husband. 'Years ago, the young people here used to go in for midnight swims, now they're afraid it might ruin their hairdos. Today nobody lives like it's the mountains.'

Finally, two lingering memories of the Sullivan County Catskills.

As I left the Laurels I actually saw a young couple lying under a sun lamp by the heated indoor pool on a day that was nice enough for swimming in the lake outside the picture window.

At Brown's, where THERE'S MORE OF EVERYTHING, a considerable number of guests ignored the endless run of facilities to sit on the balcony that overlooked the highway and watch the cars go by, the people come and go. Obviously, there's still nothing like the front-door stoop as long as passers-by know that you don't have to sit there, that you can afford everything inside.

This Year in Jerusalem

Outside, it was balmy, marvellously bright and blue; and what with London's sodden skies and bone-chilling damp only eight hours behind me, I began to feel elated. The shuttlebus to Tel Aviv, a Volkswagen, was driven by a rotund Ethiopian Jew. 'How do you like it in Israel?' he asked immediately.

'I only just got here,' I said.

The other passenger in the bus, an American boy with buckteeth, said, 'I've been here for three days. Leaving tomorrow. Tonight I'm going to see *Breakfast At Tiffany's*.'

'Did you come all this way to see movies?' I asked.

'But it's a very good movie. I'm on a world tour, you know.'

On the Allenby Road, boys and girls in uniform, kids with transistors clapped to their ears, lottery-ticket sellers, youngsters wearing tiny knitted skullcaps fastened to their heads with a bobby pin, passed to and fro. At the corner of Ben Yehudah, a young man leaned against an MG spitting out poppy seeds. The wizened street vendors, the fruit juice and bagel men, all looked Arabic to me. Actually, most of them were North African Jews. Two American ladies with winged sunglasses and gaily-patterned skirts passed with a click-clack of bracelets.

'But have you heard their English yet, Sadie?'

'No.'

'So help me, they speak better than us. They speak like the British.'

The Yiddish restaurant I stopped at was typical of its kind anywhere. Wine-stained linen tablecloths and toothpicks in brandy glasses, the familiar sour shuffling old waiter with his shirt-tail hanging out, and here and there satisfied men sucking their teeth absently. 'Sit down,' somebody said. It was Mr. Berman, who had sat immediately in front of me on the flight from London. 'This is your first time in Israel?'

'Yes it is,' I said, excited.

'All cities are the same, you know. A main street . . . hotels, restaurants . . . and everybody out to clip you. Here they're champion clippers. Me, I'm in sporting goods. I sell guns, sleeping bags, tents.' He laughed, wiped his spoon on the edge of the tablecloth, and began to chop his strawberries in sour cream. 'You'd never catch me spending a night in a sleeping bag. People are crazy. I should complain.' Mr. Berman told me he was leaving for Tokyo tomorrow. 'The girls in Tokyo are the best. They're ugly but you can get used to them. Used to them? It's easy. They wait on you hand and foot.'

Bill Arad, an Israeli acquaintance, took me to the California, a café favoured by young journalists and artists. I told him I intended to look up Uri Avnery, the editor of *Ha'Olem Haze*.

'He's a pornographer,' Arad said. 'Clever, but irresponsible. Don't believe anything he tells you about Israel.'

Arad introduced me to another journalist. Shlomo. 'Do you really call yourself "Mordecai" in Canada?' Shlomo asked, making it sound like an act of defiance.

'But it's my name,' I said, feeling stupid.

'Really? In Canada! Isn't that nice!'

The American boy with buck teeth was waiting at the bus stop. 'How was the movie?' I asked.

'It was really something. I'm on a world tour, you know.'

'You told me.'

'I leave for Bombay at three o'clock tomorrow afternoon.'

What's playing in Bombay, man? But I didn't say it. Instead, I said, 'Enjoy yourself.'

'I'll only be there overnight.'

It was not yet midnight; I decided to give the Hotel Avia's Jet Club, Open Nightly, a whirl. The bartender turned out to be a painter and an admirer of Uri Avnery. 'The government', he said, 'would rather hang him than Eichmann. Shimon Peres hates him.'

Peres, then Assistant Minister of Defence, was one of Avnery's targets. It was *Ha'Olem Haze* (This World) that first revealed Israeli-made guns were being used by the Portuguese against the natives in Angola. The bartender was distressed because, to his mind, Israel had become identified in the Middle East with repressive colonial powers. 'Uri', he said, 'was the only journalist here with guts enough to come out for an independent Algeria. The other papers stuck by France and the alliance.'

The bartender assured me that Israel kept a cultural attaché in Stockholm whose sole purpose was to lobby for a Nobel Prize for S. Y. Agnon. 'Buber would have got one last year,' he said, 'but Hammerskjold died as he was translating him.'

Each country its own cultural problems. Retiring to my room, I read in the *Herald-Tribune* that Chicago had taken Montreal in the third game of the Stanley Cup semi-finals. Mikita had figured in four goals. Beliveau had done nothing.

It was extremely hot. I considered taking a bath, but the sign over my sink restrained me.

HELP US TO IRRIGATE THE NEGEV!
SAVE WATER!
Public Committee For Water Saving

I couldn't sleep, so thrilled was I to be in Israel. Eretz Yisrael. Even the tourist office handout, *A Visitor's Guide To Israel*, had a characteristic warmth to it. 'Let's hope not, but should you require medical attention such services are easily obtainable. . . .' All my life I seem to have been heading for, and postponing, my trip to Israel. In 1936, when I was five years old, my maternal grandfather, a hasidic rabbi, bought land in Holy Jerusalem. He intended for all of us to immigrate. He died, we didn't go. When I was in high school I joined Habonim, the Labour-Zionist youth movement. On Friday evenings we listened to impassioned speeches about soil redemption, we saw movies glorifying life on the kibbutz, and danced the hora until our bodies ached. Early Sunday mornings we were out ringing doorbells for the Jewish National Fund, shaking tin boxes under uprooted sleepy faces, righteously demanding quarters, dimes, and nickels to help reclaim our desert in Eretz. Our choir sang stirring songs at fund-raising rallies. In the summertime we went to a camp in a mosquito-ridden Laurentian valley, heard more speakers, studied Hebrew and, in the absence of Arabs, watched out for fishy-looking French Canadians.

When fighting broke out in Israel, following the Proclamation of Independence on May 14, 1948, I lied about my age and joined the Canadian Reserve Army, thinking how rich it would be to have Canada train me to fight the British in Eretz, but in the end I decided to finish high school instead.

If I could put what I felt about Israel into one image I would say the news photo of Ben-Gurion, taken on his arrival in Canada. It shows that grumpy knot of a Polish Jew reviewing an honour guard of Canadian Grenadier Guards. The Guards are standing rigidly at attention; Ben-Gurion's tangle of white hair hardly comes up to their chests. I have held on to that photograph because of the immense satisfaction it gives me.

Driving into Tel Aviv the next morning we slowed down for donkey-carts and motorcycle trucks, weaving through streets of machine shops and junk yards, where I saw rusty wheels and dilapidated bedspreads, all being thriftily reclaimed. It was hot, oppressively hot, and most people, very sensibly, I thought, were informally dressed. Not so the hasidic Jews, who clung to costumes more appropriate to their East European origins; streimels and kaftans and heavy woollen sweaters. Beggars lolled in the shade of the municipal synagogue. There was a man with his trousers hitched up to reveal his artificial legs and another with a hideously gnarled face.

I stopped at a cafe on Ahad Ha-Am Street. Ahad Ha-Am ('one of the people') was the pseudonym of Asher Zvi Ginsberg, an original Zionist thinker. When he settled in Tel Aviv in his later years, the street on which he lived was named after him and even closed off during his afternoon rest hours. Ahad Ha-Am died in 1927 and today his street is a busy commercial one. Suddenly I was caught up in a swirl of shrieking newspaper vendors. '*M'ariv! M'ariv!*' I bought a copy of the *Jerusalem Post*, and was immediately struck by a boxed notice on page one.

> We have lost our crowning glory!
>   The great rabbi
>   Nissim Benjamin Phanna
> Chief Rabbi of the City of Haifa and its
> environs, has been taken by his maker
>
> Funeral cortège will leave the Rothschild
> Hospital, Haifa (April 1, 1962) 11 A.M.
>   THE BEREAVED FAMILY

Once, impassioned Russian and Polish Jews, who were determined to settle in Palestine, made up the bulk of the country's Jewish population. Now each immigrant group presents Israel with a ready-made issue. It is accepted, for instance, that many of the new arrivals from Eastern Europe were not so anxious to come to Israel as to quit the communist states. Israel is often only a transit station for them in the yearned-for trip to America. In recent years the racial structure of the country has altered drastically. Today, Kurds, North Africans, and Yemenites, who were forced – or, if you accept the Arab argument, urged by Zionist agents – to leave their homelands, account for more than a third of the population, many of them having been literally lifted – 'upon eagled wings', as in the Yemenite prophecy – from one age slap into another. The oriental Jews create Israel's thorniest social problem. Many are unskilled. Others become quickly embittered. For there's no doubt that almost all high offices in the land are filled by Western Jews. They are the managers and executives and government officials. The Kurds, Moroccans, and Yemenites tend to become labourers, army non-coms, and clerks. The army, by mixing young people of all origins into the same units, hopes to break down suspicion and prejudice, but there is already a colour problem in Israel.

Arad and I talked about the problem as we strolled toward the new Hagana Museum. 'I'm paying for it,' he said. 'We might as well look inside.'

Like most men of his generation, Arad fought first alongside the British, in World War II, and then against them in the Israeli War of Independence. We saw Orde Wingate's uniform on display in the museum. We also looked at many of the devices that were used to conceal arms in the run to Jerusalem during the siege: an oxygen tank, three rifles inside, a boiler stuffed with a machine gun, and other seemingly innocuous agricultural equipment, all used to hide arms. I also saw my first Davidka.

When morale in Jerusalem was possibly at its lowest, as the shelling of the Holy City reached such a pitch that the projectiles were falling at the rate of one every two minutes and the Jews inside had nothing to reply with, a young engineer, David Leibovitch, invented a home-made weapon that came to be known as the Davidka. Dov Joseph, in *The Faithful City*, writes, 'It was basically a kind of mortar that used a six-inch drainpipe. It fired a bomb of nails and metal scrap which exploded with some force and – what was more important – with tremendous noise and fury. Its effect on the

Arabs was sometimes considerable . . . its noise frightened them almost as much as its projectiles hurt them, and it gave great heart to the people of Jerusalem when real artillery shells were falling on them.'

On Sunday I moved to the Garden Hotel in Ramat Aviv. On the way to my bungalow I passed the pool, where lots of foot-weary, middle-aged tourists were sunning themselves.

'The ones I saw in Jerusalem they're poor kids,' a lady said. 'They don't even know what a handkerchief is, should I chase them away? They're sneezing and blowing and coughing all the time.'

A card player looked up from under his baseball cap long enough to say he was taking the tour to Eilat tomorrow.

'If you're constipated,' Mr. Ginsburg told him, 'the water is good for you, if not – pardon me the expression – you'll get the diarrhoea.'

Mr. Ginsburg questioned each new arrival at the hotel. Shooing flies away with his rolled newspaper, pondering his toes as he curled and uncurled them, he'd ask, 'And where are *you* from? Ah ha . . . How long you here for? I see . . . Longer you couldn't stay? . . . And tell me, Mr. Richler, you came over here on one of our planes, you like it? You were impressed?'

'They're Boeing 707s, you know. American-made.'

'And the pilots? Eh? . . . This country it's a miracle. . . . So? The only thing I got a complaint is the hotel keepers they make the monkey business. I been here seven years ago and what they done since it's remarkable. . . . I'm not a millionaire, Mr. Richler, and I'm not poor. I spend? It's the children's money. . . . Do I want to be the richest man in the cemetery? The less I leave, the less the children have to fight over, God bless them. So, Mr. Richler, you're enjoying here?'

Sitting on the terrace of a café on the Dizengoff Street in the afternoon, I saw a crazed young man pass reading aloud from a Hebrew prayer book. Drifting up and down there was the inevitable spill of young officers and smart-looking girls in uniforms. An elderly hassid shuffled from table to table, selling plastic combs, toothbrushes, and religious articles. Later, Bill Arad joined me. He told me of how success had changed the kibbutzim. Once, he said, there had been fierce ideological arguments as to whether it was a bourgeois corruption to replace the benches with chairs in the communal dining hall. Now people took their evening meal in the privacy of their own cabins. The kibbutz movement was dying, very few new ones were being started.

Arad and I drifted to the California, where we fell in with two young architects. One of them felt that the Eichmann trial was a mistake. 'It dragged on and on, cheapening things.'

'But we had to have a trial to educate the young. They have no respect. They don't understand why the Jews in Europe didn't rebel.'

'We're a new kind of Jew here,' the other architect said. 'What do you think?'

The other side of Ramla, our bus began the slow winding rise and fall, rise and fall, through the bony, densely cultivated mountains. Arab villages jutted natural and ravaged as rock out of the hills. The gutted shells of armoured trucks lay overturned round bends in the narrow steepening road. Here a dried wreath hung on a charred chassis; elsewhere mounds of stone marked where a driver, trapped in the cab of his burning truck, had died an excruciating death. These ruins, spilling along the roadside, were a memorial to those who had been killed running the blockade into Jerusalem in April, 1948, when the Arabs held the vital heights of Bab el Wad and Kastel, an ancient Roman encampment and crusaders' castle which dominate the closest approaches to the city.

I took a taxi to the Hebrew University. On the way, we passed a prison block. 'Today he's in there,' the driver said.

'Who?'

'The Eichmann.'

With Yizhok, a law clerk who had just completed a month's military duty on the Jerusalem frontier, I climbed a stony hill to an abandoned courtyard where the Israelis and Jordanians occupied sandbagged positions about a hundred yards apart. 'When I served here,' Yizhok said, 'we used to gossip every morning and throw fruit back and forth.'

From the lookout at Ramat Chen, Yizhok pointed out Mount Zion, the road to Bethlehem, the hill where Solomon's Tomb is supposed to be and, baking in the distance, the Old City of Jerusalem.

Mr. Ginsburg was lying in wait for me in the lobby of the Garden Hotel.

'Tell me, Mr. Richler, is it right I have donated so much to build this country . . . it costs a man thousands to come here . . . is it right they should charge me extra if I want a cup tea after my dinner?'

I assured him hotel keepers were the same everywhere. They would charge him extra for his tea in Italy too.

'Italy,' he said, disgusted.

I told Uri Avnery about Mr. Ginsburg. 'He feels unwanted in Israel,' I said.

Avnery replied, 'But for the middle-aged tourists from America, the old-time Zionists, this has to be paradise and no criticism is possible. They come here as to heaven on earth and they want it pure, not filled with quarrelling human beings. Those old men would cut off their fingers for Israel. It's true they wouldn't settle here, but they will pay for it. They are, in a sense, the backbone of the Israeli economy.' Yet, he felt, many Israelis were anti-Jewish. 'As far as most people are concerned your middle-aged tourists are shirkers for living abroad. They come here to be delighted by Jewish cops, a Jewish army, well, they have to pay for it.'

Avnery's office was bombed twice. He has been beaten up.

He described his weeky, *Ha'Olem Haze*, as one-third sex and sensation, one-third *Time*-style, and another third modelled on *l'Expresse*. 'Ours is the only true opposition paper,' he said.

When *Ha'Olem Haze* revealed that Israeli arms were being used in Angola, the report was denied by the government. But Avnery insisted and other, more reputable, journals were obliged to investigate the claim. They came back with concrete proof that a number of Israeli-made arms were in fact being used in Angola. 'The government', Avnery said, 'then explained they had sold the arms to Germany and had no idea where or how they would be used. That much is true. But what is also true is they must have known Germany had no need whatsoever for Israeli arms. . . . They buy them for show, out of guilt. . . . Also they are too clever to send their own arms for use in a dirty colonial war. So,' he said, 'once more we get the worst of both worlds.'

We drove past Ben-Gurion's house. Ben-Gurion, who was then still prime minister, had three homes. An official residence in Jerusalem, his own house in Tel Aviv, and his desert retreat. 'He really hates the desert,' Avnery said, 'but he is a man with a rare sense of style. If he is going to be interviewed on American TV he flies out to the desert by helicopter a half hour before the camera crew. A half hour after they've left he's back in Tel Aviv.' Avnery spoke of Ben-Gurion with warmth. 'Nobody here can touch him politically.'

The Israeli economy, Avnery argued, was totally unrealistic. It was based on continued help from Zionists outside the country, international loans, and German reparation money. 'Israel insists on behaving as if it was not a Middle Eastern country. The Jews will continue to pretend they are a Western power. Nobody is really interested in what goes on in Alexandria and Beirut, so close by, but they will go rushing off to New York and London, where they can parade as heroes in the Jewish communities. . . . From the beginning, going back to the days of the earliest settlements, there has never been an attempt to assimilate with the Arabs.'

Finally, Avnery said. 'You know, I love it here.' He had to laugh at himself. 'In London, where you live, everything's been done. Here, we'll see.'

Hadera, a sun-baked industrial town on the coastal plain had the rare distinction, for Israel, of not being listed as 'a place of interest' in any official guide book I'd seen. Only an hour's run from Tel Aviv along the coastal plan, the town is built on sand dunes. My cousin Shmul lived there.

I had not seen Shmul since we had both been kids together in Montreal, more than twenty years ago. Shmul's shop, the Hadera Locksmithy, was shut down. He wasn't home, either. But his wife, Sarah, let me into their apartment. Sarah was a New Yorker. She and Shmul kept a strictly orthodox home. They had met on a kibbutz, on their first trip to Israel some years ago, and then again in New York, where they were married and had a child. Shmul had learnt his locksmith's trade in New York, bought equipment on credit and returned to settle in Hadera with his family. I asked Sarah about the Moroccan Jews I had seen on the street.

'A problem? Wherever you have black and white there's a problem. With the least excuse,' she said, 'they take out a knife. . . . The worst are the ones from the Atlas Mountains. They've just come out of the caves.'

Sarah went next door to phone another cousin of mine, Benjy, who taught at a school in Parness Channa, close by. I hadn't seen Benjy since his bar mitzvah, eight years ago. He had grown into a tall thin introverted boy. A knitted skullcap was clasped to his head with a bobby pin; he wore a beard. Benjy explained why he had quit Canada. 'I would always think that one day I'd have to leave, all the Jews would have to leave. It's not our country.'

Benjy took me to a liquor store where I could buy a bottle of cognac to take back to Shmul's house. Benjy interrupted the transaction. 'Is this bottle kosher?' he demanded of the shopkeeper.

'Don't worry,' the shopkeeper said impatiently, 'it's kosher, it's kosher.'

Orthodox Jews are not enormously popular in Israel. They are considered a throwback to the ghetto. I asked Benjy if he thought the religious community had an influence out of proportion to its numbers on the secular life in the country. 'Elsewhere,' he said, 'I would be for a separation of church and state, but this is Israel. If civil marriage was allowed there would eventually be two nations.'

Sarah, like so many of the Americans and Canadians I met who had settled in Israel, retained a reserve of arrogance about the gesture. 'Don't forget we didn't have to come here. Like the European Jews.'

My Cousin Shmul no longer called himself Herscovitch. He had, following a popular immigrant practice, given his name a clearer Israeli ring. He was known as Shmul Shimshoni.

'When I first came to Hadera,' he said, 'the locals thought I was crazy. For forty years, they said, there has never been a locksmith in town, what do we need one now for? Then, out of sympathy for a new man, one by one they looked for something in their attics to bring into my shop. My first customer brought me an old suitcase, the case was locked and the key was lost, he asked if I could open it and make him a new key. When I did it for him, he was amazed. He had to go home to get money to pay me. . . . Over here, we believe in letting the other man live. As long as you're not a pig, everybody helps out.'

I returned to Jerusalem on Friday to assemble with two hundred others to hear a lecture by Y. Freiman and join the synagogue tour to Mea Shearim. Our group, predominantly American, was composed of gaudily made-up middle-aged women and their cigar-biting men, harnessed with cameras, light meters, filters, and binoculars. Freiman, speaking above a jangle of bracelets and winding cameras, reminded us that in ancient times the priests and Levites, dressed in white, used to make the pilgrimage to Jerusalem at just this time of year, between Purim and Passover. The tradition of a sabbath eve visit to Jerusalem went back to the time of Solomon's Temple.

Only Yiddish is spoken in Mea Shearim; Hebrew, the holy language, being restricted to prayers. The devout Jews of Jerusalem used to live in the Old City, close by the Wailing Wall, but after the war in 1948 they were forced to take up residence in Mea Shearim, outside the Old City walls. The predominant influence in the quarter is Polish, but other, equally devout groups are of Persian, Yemenite, and North African extraction. Rivalry is fierce. Yemenites will not eat meat slaughtered by Polish hassids, and vice versa. One might expect that all groups were at least united by dint of their shared wait for the Messiah, but even here there is cause for dispute. The Yemenites are sure that when the Messiah comes he will be a dark Jew; the Poles insist he will surely be white, like themselves. The Jews of Mea Shearim are agreed on only one issue: none of them recognizes the state of Israel. In a typically virulent sermon Rabbi Binyamin Mendelson said, 'Zionism and nationalism were responsible for the Nazi holocaust. Zionism prevented the coming of the Messiah, which would have saved Jewry.'

Following Mr. Freiman's lecture we set out in buses for the narrow, squalid streets of Mea Shearim. It was an unusually hot afternoon. Poor men with glazed eyes watched as our group shuffled past, others slammed their doors as we approached. You could hardly blame them. More than once a tourist would stop, push open the door to somebody else's home, and beckon to his wife, 'Look, Sylvia, it's not so bad inside.'

A man clad in dirty pyjamas sat on a stone outside his house, muttering to himself. Another man, more sprightly, hurried from street to street, blowing on a horn to announce the approach of the sabbath. One of our number, a fat lady with sunglasses, poked our guide with a dimpled elbow and pointed to an olive-skinned little girl playing on a square. 'Is *that one* Jewish?' she demanded.

'Oh, yes,' the guide said, 'She's from Persia.'

'Isn't that nice, Irving?'

Irving stopped, grinned at the retreating child, and called out. '*Shabbat shalom.*'

As we twisted up yet another cramped, narrow alley, a man said to his wife, 'I'll bet you couldn't buy a lot here for any price.'

'Who wants one?' she replied.

Inside one small dank synagogue, God's name was spelled out in neon lights over the Holy Ark. In the Yemenite *shul*, the last one we visited, the guide announced, 'In this synagogue, the rabbi will come out and bless *all of you.*'

A decrepit old man, wearing a fez, came out and muttered a prayer.

'*You have now been blessed,*' the guide said. 'Anybody who wants to shake hands with the rabbi is now free to do so. One further announcement. Please do not rush for the buses. There are enough seats for everybody.'

Tovia Shlonsky, a young lecturer at the Hebrew University, told me how much he admired Bellow, Malamud, Roth. 'Unfortunately, they are not much read here.' He laughed, embarrassed. 'The young think of them as ghetto writers.'

Tovia picked me up at noon Saturday and we went to visit a young couple he knew who had just built a house in Abu-Tor, on the frontier with Jordan, overlooking an Arab village on the mountainside and the walled Old City. As we sat on the terrace, sipping Turkish coffee, we could hear the Arabs on the other side of the frontier being summoned to prayer. 'At night we can listen to their drummers,' Miriam said. 'Children often stray across the frontier. The Arabs are very good about it. They always give the kids candy, treat them well, and return them. But if an adult wanders across, he's beaten up. Not gratuitously,' she added. 'For information.'

Miriam, like most intellectuals I met, wanted more traffic with the Arabs. She missed her old Moslem neighbours and regretted that Jerusalem had not been made an international city.

A youth group, wearing blue hats, neckerchiefs, shorts, and carrying packs, marched past below, singing vigorously. 'Just consider our splendid view,' Miriam said. 'We can see the Old City, the Arabs . . . but the poor Arabs,' she said, indicating the singing group below, 'this is all they can see.'

'I'm putting up the finest hotel in Israel,' Raphael Elan told me, 'the biggest hotel in the desert. It's in Beersheba – the Desert Inn. We're going to have a golf course, hot springs – the works. I'm even organizing a secret international society to be called Sons of the Desert.'

Elan was a squat, thrusting man in his late thirties. His project was backed by Canadian and American capital. 'It isn't charity, it's business. Either we show a profit or die.'

Elan came round early Monday morning in an American station wagon to drive me to Beersheba. With him were a Lieutenant-Colonel in the Air Force, Mischa Keren, and two hotel employees, a Mrs. Raphaeli and a Mr. Gordon. About a half hour out of Tel Aviv, we wheeled inland into a lush cultivated belt. 'When I used to fly over this area in 48–49,' Keren said, 'it was almost impossible to navigate. It was all desert. Look how green it is now.'

Elan, an endless run of statistics at his command, went on and on about irrigation, reclamation, and crops. He was tiresome; but the accomplishment was clearly impressive, especially once we started into the desert proper and I could see how desolate the greenery had once been.

'You have no idea what a pleasure it is for me', Keren said, 'to see women and children walking casually along the highway.' Before the Sinai campaign, he said, it was impossible, for this was the area where the *fedayin* used to strike regularly.

We started into the tribal hills of Sheik Suleiman, an encampment that went on for miles, darkened here and there by long low black tents made from sheepskins. Suleiman, a Bedouin chief, was loyal to Israel during the war, and for this he had been rewarded with tractors, land grants, and other aid: he had also become something of a standing joke in the country. The Bedouin land, on one side of the highway, looked parched, compared to the kibbutz fields on the other. 'The Bedouins', Elan said, 'are not interested in irrigation, which can take years to pay off. Instead of investing in the land they bury their money in jars in the earth.' As we cut deeper into a landscape of blowing sands, gritty shrubs and dunes, Keren added, 'This must be our breadbasket one day. This is where our country is widest.'

We rocked to a stop on the outskirts of Beersheba. Protecting my face against windblown sand, I saw an enormous roadhouse rising abruptly out of the desert. 'This is it,' Elan said. 'Later we'll have the biggest neon sign in Israel – THE DESERT INN – and you'll be able to spot us from miles away.'

A chauffeured car was parked alongside us. The foreman was showing a middle-aged American couple through the inn. 'More stockholders,' Elan said, irritated. But once he caught up with Dr. and Mrs. Edelson he was ready with a smile. 'Hi.'

'Say, you've got a quite a baby here.'

'Have you seen anything like it anywhere in Israel?'

'Quite a baby, I'd say.'

'On the execution side and the investment side,' Elan said, 'this is the most modern hotel in Israel. The best.'

We moved out of the blowing sand into a litter of planks, piping and puddles, that was to be the dining-room. 'The sweeping suspended stairway, the only one of its kind in Israel, will be right here.'

Dr. Edelson walked to the edge to look.

'Oh, I can see you could sell anything,' Mrs. Edelson said, 'but it's quite a baby, isn't it, Henry?'

'It's my baby I'm selling.'

'Don't you worry. You know how they say "Next Year in Jerusalem"? Well, we'll be saying "Next year at the Desert Inn", won't we, Henry?'

Sidestepping wet cement and exposed nails, Elan led us inside an unfinished suite. '*Shalom, shalom,*' Dr. Edelson sang out warmly to the men at work. Then, turning to Elan, he said, 'They don't seem to work very fast here, do they?' Mrs. Edelson stopped, her brow wrinkled, before some nudes that had been drawn in pencil on the framework of the bathroom door. 'I suppose,' she said, 'this does come off . . . ?'

'Sure, sure, like to see the roof?' As he led us through more muck into the second wing of the inn, Elan said, 'We were not going to build this wing for another two years, then the demand for reservations was so high – '

'You hear, Henry?'

' – that we decided it would be best to *build big* before another hotel opened across the road.'

We emerged in front of the inn again.

'I'm going to have a doorman with a long sword standing here. The waitresses will wear veils.'

Elan took us to see the unfinished Sheik's Suite.

'You know what it says up there,' Mrs. Edelson said with a smile. 'It says reserved for Dr. and Mrs. Edelson.'

'Want to make reservations. Speak to Mrs. Raphaeli.'

'Oh, good . . . em, what will stockholders have to pay when you open up?'

'Stockholders will be allowed to sign for one month's credit. Like to see our kitchens?'

'We want to see *everything*. But . . . em, what will stock-holders have to pay?'

Dr. Edelson pretended to be winding his camera.

'In the United States,' Mrs. Edelson continued, 'if you bring a guest and you're a stockholder, well, once a month the guest is free. . . . It's very nice, you know. *It makes for good-will.*'

At last Elan led the Edelsons to their car.

'Well, I'm sure you'll want to put out the red carpet for us when you open, *won't you, Mr. Elan?*'

'Sure will.'

'Next year at the Desert Inn.'

We stopped at a Rumanian restaurant in Beersheba for lunch. Lieutenant-Colonel Keren, who had flown for the Red Air Force in World War II, told me that as a young man in Russia he had hardly known or cared that he was a Jew. 'When I came home after the war I found that all my family was dead. Sudden outbursts of anti-Semitism here and there made me feel uncomfortable. I decided to get out. Israel was an accident, though. I might just as easily have gone to America. But I came here and I feel good. I did not feel good in Russia. I'm not what you would call a Zionist, but I feel good here.'

I asked Keren about the Arabs.

'We're only twenty miles wide. Either we live in Israel or we drown in the sea. So we will fight very hard and they must know it.' Still, he was troubled about the refugees on the Gaza Strip. 'The way they live; it's terrible. But we have only twenty miles and then the sea. Why can't Nasser help them? We help our refugees. You saw the houses we built for them.'

Mr. Gordon and Mrs. Raphaeli had other problems.

'It will be difficult for us to hire waiters,' Mrs. Raphaeli said.

I asked why.

'Jews don't want to be waiters. Head waiters yes.'

'Maybe some Yemenites,' Mrs. Raphaeli suggested.

'We're going to have trouble.'

Finally, we drove off. As we passed Sheik Suleiman's camp once more, Elan said, 'I've got quite a deal with Suleiman. I'm going to take the Sons of the Desert for treks into his camp at night. They'll see Bedouin dances, eat in tents – the works. Only trouble is the camp is too close. I'll have to lead the Sons in circles on the back roads to make them think they've come a long way.'

Returning to Tel Aviv, we drove through Rishon-le-Zion, the first agricultural settlement in Israel founded by the Bilu pioneers late in the 19th century.

'My grandfather was a Bilu,' Elan said.

'A real Mayflower type, our Elan,' Mr. Gordon said.

We had to slow down to a crawl as we approached the big brilliantly-lit sprawl of Tel Aviv. 'Well, well, well,' Mrs. Raphaeli said, 'I can still remember when Tel Aviv was only a street.'

'Even when I first came here,' Elan said, 'we were just a family. Today we're a nation.'

Of all the places I had seen in Israel, I came to feel most at ease in Tel Aviv. It was not nearly as beautiful as Haifa. It hadn't, like Jerusalem, a halo of history suspended above. Tel Aviv was a dirty, grubby Mediterranean city, but livelier and with more spirit than any other place I had been to in the country.

One evening, a couple of weeks after I arrived in Israel, I was invited to a dinner party in honour of a celebrated left-wing theatre director from London and the Ambassador from Ghana. Racial relations took an embarrassing turn early – the director, her eyes brimful of love, told the Ambassador, 'Your people are natural actors' – then broke down completely when the director asked the Ambassador 'to sing us a song'.

Retreating hastily to another room, I fell in with Migdal. Migdal, a thin severe man in his sixties, came of a French-

Jewish family. A graduate in engineering from the Ecole Polytechnique, he first came to Palestine with the Foreign Legion in the Twenties. There he met and married a Canadian girl, quit the Legion, and swiftly established himself as a consultant engineer and agent for British firms in Palestine, Transjordan and Syria. Migdal was equally at ease in French, Hebrew, English and four Arabic tongues. He returned to France in 1939, fought first with the French army and then with the British as a colonel. Still later he commanded a sector of Jerusalem during the seige.

Migdal turned out to dislike American Jews more vehemently than most. 'This country', he said, 'restored Jewish pride with the defence of Jerusalem and then bartered it for American-Jewish aid. We can do without the fancy new Hebrew University, we didn't need the hideous Rabbinate building in Jerusalem. We could wait another ten years for such things, until we could properly afford them.'

Migdal was full of contempt for the hassids of Mea Shearim.

'No sooner had the Arabs attacked than they were ready with the white flag. You'll find we're a new kind of Jew here. We don't cringe.'

'I didn't come all the way to Israel,' I said, 'to hear that familiar anti-Semitic argument. The Jews in Canada didn't cringe either, when it was time to go to war.'

'There are only two possibilities for the Jew,' Migdal said. 'Assimilate or come to Israel. Nothing else will do.'

I asked Migdal if it was possible that the concept of a nation-state, with all it entailed, was contrary to the real Jewish tradition.

'If you mean', he said, 'that we have compromised our lousy Jewish souls here then you're right. This state deals, lies, and cheats, just like any other. But we have restored Jewish pride. It's worth it.'

Mr. Ginsburg was back. He had been to Haifa for a couple

of days. 'So, Mr. Richler, walk, walk, see, see. Quite a country, eh?'

'Mr. Ginsburg,' I said, 'we're surrounded by anti-Semites here.'

'Ah-ha. So you drink a little, Richler?'

'Yes. But we're surrounded by anti-Semites all the same. Ever read Koestler?'

'Who?'

'*Darkness At Noon*. When Rubashov is in prison, as they march him up and down the yard for afternoon exercise, the crazed man behind him, another old Bolshevik, repeats over and over again, "This could never happen in a socialist country." Rubashov hasn't the heart to tell him they're actually in Russia.'

'Very interesting. But this . . . Koestler; he's a communist?'

'He used to sell lemonade right here in Tel Aviv.'

'Oh, that's something else. That's different.'

Following the example of the tourists who had come to see heaven on earth and wanted it pure, not filled with quarrelling human beings, I often did not go out but lay exhausted by the poolside. Half-asleep, I used to hear their voices.

'If I send a letter to my Stuart in Toronto do I have to write "Canada" too?'

'What are you wearing tonight – the long sleeves or the short?'

From another nest of canvas chairs.

'Do you know how long this hotel would last in Miami?'

'What?'

'Six days – and boom, bankrupt. The waiter didn't even bring me a glass of water with my meal.'

These people, not surprisingly soured by an accumulation of strange bed, bumpy drives, haggling tourist agents, and unaccustomed foods; these people, clearly dejected because not flowers but scorn was thrown in their path in Israel, had, it suddenly occurred to me, done more real good than I ever had. Tiresome, vulgar, rude they might be, but the flawed reality of Israel was a testimony to their generosity. Evidence of their achievement was everywhere. Hospitals, factories, forests, libraries, schools, mostly paid for out of tin boxes in corner groceries as well as the big donations pledged in the heady atmosphere of the country club.

Tovia Shlonsky had once said, 'Why shouldn't they pay for Israel? Their money is ill-begotten anyway.'

If it's ill-begotten, why accept it? And ill-begotten or not there was no reason why they had to give the money to Israel. Whatever their motives – community pressure, the need for prestige, tax exemptions – the result was the same; and they could just as easily have blown the money on a fling.

One afternoon an old settler said to me, 'Why should we feel obligated because of American-Jewish patronage? It's blood money they give us. We risk our lives here. They're paying off their guilt for not coming here.'

'We need Anglo-Saxons urgently,' Mr. Chaifetz said, at the annual dinner of the Association of Americans and Canadians in Israel, at the Sheraton Hotel.

It is one of the smaller ironies of Israeli life that immigrants from Canada, England, and the U.S.A., who often left their countries because the Anglo-Saxons there made them feel unwanted, are, in Israel, called Anglo-Saxons themselves. All Canadian and American settlers can and generally do retain dual citizenship – a possible out in hard times that has antagonized other Israelis. Canadian and American settlers are in fact regarded with scepticism. Too many return when they find the going difficult.

One afternoon I called on Murray Greenfield, director of the Association of Americans and Canadians in Israel. Greenfield, an explosively energetic man of thirty-six, came to Israel in 1947 to serve with Hagana, and now, his work for the

Association apart, he ran two art galleries and was active in real estate. 'Half the Canadians and Americans who come here leave after two-three years,' he said. 'If they stay longer they're hooked. Why do they quit? They think it's all going to be orange picking and dancing the hora. They go to a kibbutz and want to dance round a tree after one bushel's been picked. Another reason so many go home is, let's face it, most of them come from middle-class homes and coming here means a big drop in their standard of living. Not everybody can take it. Many others miss their close family ties. Momma.'

In recent years, Aliyah from Canada and the U.S.A. had dropped to a trickle; it could be measured in hundreds.

'I'm a big fish in a small pond,' Greenfield said, 'and I like it. You know, my picture's in the papers here, everybody knows who I am. I'm taking part in something. In America who knows me? Who would care?'

Greenfield, along with other Anglo-Saxon settlers, including Meyer Levin, was trying to start a reform synagogue in Tel Aviv: his group was worried about anti-Americanism in the country. 'This could still become an independent non-Jewish sort of state rather than a centre for world Judaism.'

At Greenfield's art gallery, in the Sheraton Hotel, we ran into the fabulous Brother John, a California millionaire whose holdings included a vast cattle ranch, uranium mines and chemical plants. Brother John was one of a breed of Bible-reading Gentiles who wanted to take part in the rebirth of the Holy Land.

Brother John came of a long tradition. In 1844, the United States sent its first representative to Palestine, accrediting Mr. Warden Cressen as first U.S. Consul to the Turkish Court and 'All the Holy Land'. Cressen established himself in Jerusalem and a year later embraced Judaism and changed his name to Michael Boaz Israel. In 1847, Israel founded an agricultural colony, 'God's Vineyard', on the outskirts of Jerusalem. Employing the Bible as a text and his own farming experience as a guide, Israel printed pamphlets and sought volunteers for his project. Within four years two hundred Americans joined him, fifty-two were Jewish and the others converts to Judaism or Protestants. The colony, born before its time, sank into oblivion, but not the tradition.

Brother John, the most engaging of tycoons, had made it his personal mission to replenish the zoos of the Holy Land, flying in once or twice a year with the gift of a giraffe or perhaps an elephant. He had already dropped thousands in zany Israeli investments, but he was not dismayed. 'I have just earned my first Israeli dividend.' Brother John, a prodigious Bible student, had invested in a new chemical plant in an unpromising area because he remembered Moses had said, 'Judah will dig riches from the earth here.' Brother John banged his gold-tipped walking stick against a chair, he waved his stock certificate at us. 'And by George they have, they sure have!'

Greenfield and I retired to the MacCabean Room at the Sheraton Hotel, where a quartet was playing a cha-cha-cha. 'We're living too high in Israel these days. It's unrealistic. But this is a crazy, lucky country. When the United Jewish Appeal money began to dry up, German reparations began.'

'What happens when that ends?'

'Another miracle, I suppose. Ask Brother John.'

On the short flight to Eilat, we flew first over the green cultivated belt so recently torn from the desert; then Beersheba. Between Beersheba and Eilat there was only sand and rock. The Negev. A desolate, ghostly landscape of dunes and red mountains and hills laced together with desiccated river beds. Just before Eilat there came Beer Ora and the copper mines that went back to King Solomon's time.

The Hotel Eilat was managed by a young Canadian, Harvey Goodman, thirty-one, who was brought up on Clark Street in Montreal, just around the corner from where I used to live.

Goodman had been in Israel for ten years. 'All Jews should come here. We're hated everywhere.'

I protested.

'Come on. How can you feel comfortable in Canada – with them? They don't want us. Me, I'm always nervous in their company. Fuck 'em.'

'Aren't you curious about Clark Street? Wouldn't you like to see it again?'

'The ghetto? Yiddish mommas? The hell.'

A pale, stooping old man approached our table timidly. It was only a day before Passover, the man was a monitor from the rabbinical council, and he had come to see whether the dietary laws were being observed. 'I could do without him,' Goodman said. 'I'd like to toss him into the sea. The bastards who come here from America don't keep kosher at home, but when they're in the Holy Land they expect us to do it for them.'

I went to watch the bronzed young fishermen haul in their nets, which were heavy with gasping, struggling Blue Fish. The fish kicked up a violent spray; soon the sea was red with their blood.

The bartender at the Hotel Eilat was a Jew from Tangier. 'One day,' he said, 'I served a Spaniard here. A rich man. He told me that in Madrid he was an anti-Semite. He said, I didn't believe these Jews could ever build a country, so I thought I'd see for myself. Well, now I've seen the country, he said, and it's marvellous. It wouldn't surprise me if you people had the atom bomb in five years and took over the Middle East in ten. But you're not Jews; you're different. You've fought for your land, you've spilled blood for it, and you have pride. The Jews in Spain would only fight for their families and their businesses. You're different here, he said,' the bartender repeated proudly.

In all the bars I had been to in Israel I had never encountered anybody who had had too much to drink, so running into glassy-eyed Bernard, a local fisherman, was something of an occasion. Unfortunately, we did not hit it off. Clapping me on the back as he ordered another round, Bernard said, 'I'm not personal, but I always speak frankly. I don't like Canadians . . . Canada is a big country, it's as small as Lichtenstein. Understand?'

'I understand. Goodman doesn't like Canada either. They hate him there.'

'You know why I live here?'

'Don't tell me. It's because you're a new kind of Jew,' I said, glaring at the bartender.

'I'm not Tolstoi, I'm not Christ,' Bernard said. 'I'm just a stinking Jew, but I like my smell.'

'You smell like a lousy fisherman to me.'

Bernard slapped me on the back again. 'I'm a Jew,' he bellowed. 'Like Freud. Like Einstein.'

'The hell you are. You're not a Jew like Freud or a fisherman like St. Peter. You're a fisherman like a fisherman, Bernard.'

'I've never liked Canadians.'

'Well, I'm a Canadian. Like Maurice Richard.'

'You're a stinking Jew. Like me.'

'I'm a Canadian Jew. That means I'll fight for my family and my business, if I had one, but not for my country.'

'I didn't say the Spaniard was right,' the bartender said. 'I only work here.'

'You tell your rich Spanish friend that the Jews in Canada have not only fought for their country – some of them even fought for Spain.'

'You're an assimilationist,' Bernard said.

'The truth is, I'm one of the Elders of Zion.'

I ended an altogether unsatisfactory evening in Eilat's one nightclub, The End of the World. A busload of Swedes had preceded me. They sat around drinking beer as two young

Israeli folksingers, wearing Yemenite shirts, sang 'Take Me Back To The Red River Valley' in Hebrew.

The Anglo-Saxon kibbutz of Gesher Haziv lies in the foothills of the Galilee, a mile from the Mediterranean, five miles from the Lebanese border: it is at the opposite end of the country from Eilat. Before flying to Eilat I had booked a taxi driver in Tel Aviv to meet my return flight and drive me to the kibbutz, eighty odd miles away, as I would be travelling on the eve of the Passover, not unlike the Christmas rush in Canada. 'How much do you want?' I asked the driver.

'Are we getting married? Do we need a rabbi? We'll settle a price tomorrow.'

We settled there and then for £50 Israeli; about seventeen dollars.

'In Canada', the driver said as we started out the next morning, 'you must have your own airplane.'

'I'm afraid not.'

'But many Canadians have private planes,' he said, affronted. 'Say, one in ten.'

'Not even one in ten thousand.'

'You think I'd charge more?' His was the usual old, battered DeSoto with shattered windows and dented fenders. 'Next to Japan,' he said proudly, 'we have the highest accident rate in the world.'

I whistled, impressed.

'And that', he added, 'is without benefit of drunken drivers. So, in Canada, you drive a Jaguar I'm sure.'

'In Canada, I once drove a taxi too. Just like you.'

'Can I pick up other people on the road? We could go partners.'

'No.'

Gesher Haziv, at first glance, suggested a summer camp in the Laurentians. A main dining hall, other administration and communal buildings, and shaded paths leading off to the cabins. The kibbutz was built on the site of an old British army rest camp in 1949 by Habonim members, drawn from Canada and the United States, in association with forty sabras. I was taken to the home of a Canadian family, Meyer and Deborah Shlossberg, where I was immediately made welcome. Capable Deborah, mother of three boys, wore trousers and men's shoes. Meyer, who was in charge of the turkey farm, came in, exhausted. 'We're expecting more than a hundred guests for the *seder*,' he said.

Passover celebrates our liberation from Egypt. At the *seder*, the father of the family reads aloud from the Haggadah, beginning, 'We were slaves in Egypt. . . .' Traditionally, the youngest member of the family asks four questions, starting with, 'Why is this night different from any other night?' For years now the kibbutz movement has been experimenting with a more militant Haggadah, a revised version which includes new Israeli songs and more recent history. But kibbutzniks have found this increasingly unsatisfactory and are gradually lapsing back towards the traditional Haggadah.

The *seder*, at Gesher Haziv, was conducted admirably by Bill Kofsky of Montreal. After the meal, there was an hour's break, allowing the children to be put to bed and the tables to be cleared. I was invited to an American couple's cabin for coffee and cake. David's wife said, 'Some things you can't modernize. You know what I miss? I miss my father's jokes.'

David and his wife worked extremely hard. I asked them if they weren't resentful of visiting freeloaders, like me.

'As long as they don't take moving pictures in the dining-room like last year we don't mind. We're not monkeys in a zoo here.'

Bill Kofsky, a reserved, intelligent man in his mid-thirties, has been at Gesher Haziv since it was founded in 1949. His wife's American; they have two children. In Gesher Haziv, children live with their families, which is a radical departure in kibbutz living, an experiment that has been closely watched by other communal farms. 'Originally,' Kofsky said, 'it was felt that we were going to create a new man for a new society and so it was necessary to protect the kids from the ghetto mentality of their parents. We might unconsciously taint them. It was best to leave them to their teachers. But somehow,' Kofsky said, fondling the child on his lap, 'it just didn't work out. Other kibbutzim would like to follow us, but it means rebuilding, they'd have to add extra rooms to the cabins, and there isn't always money.'

The one hundred and twenty founders of Gesher Haziv lived in tents for the first year. The next year, whilst they were still clearing the fields and as yet had no income, they moved into temporary shacks, and the following year they borrowed money to build their permanent dwellings. 'That was how our financial troubles started,' Deborah said. 'We're still paying interest on these houses.'

When the young, unproven kibbutz wanted to borrow money they had to resort to the black market, where interest rates were as high as thirty per cent. Further loans have been negotiated to buy equipment and against the occasional crop failure. 'The result', Kofsky said, 'is that we now put in a fifth of our working day just to pay off interest.'

Debts aside, the problems of Gesher Haziv were considerable. 'First of all,' Kofsky said, 'there's the big turnover in people. Let's say a new guy comes out here with a wife and kids, maybe we build a house for him, we certainly clothe and school his kids. It takes a new guy six months before he's any good in the fields, and all that time we lose the labour of another man, the guy who's training him. Well, O.K. But maybe six months later the guy ups and returns to Canada or moves to the city. . . . Or let's say, we decide to go in for cotton. We train a guy, he becomes our cotton expert, and a year later he moves off and we're in trouble with cotton.'

The practice of even modified socialism on the kibbutz exacts a toll. As everybody is theoretically equal on the kibbutz all members are elected to offices of authority (secretary, farm supervisor) for limited periods only. This is supposed to make for a built-in safeguard against the development of two classes: the workers and the bosses. 'But the result', Kofsky said, 'is not altogether satisfactory. It takes six months to train a secretary, a year passes, and we have to train another. We lose a lot in efficiency. Also, in spite of our efforts, we find the same personalities turning up again and again in the bigger, responsible jobs.'

Gesher Haziv, like many other kibbutzim, has been unable to make a financial success of agriculture, an industry somewhat dependent on cheap labour at harvest time, so the kibbutz was feeling its way into industry and would even hire casual labour, a definite break with kibbutz dogma. One Anglo-Saxon kibbutz, Urim, had built a knife factory: Gesher Haziv was going to manufacture turkey sausage and was hopefully building a tourist hotel. HAVE AN UNUSUAL HOLIDAY – SEE LIFE ON A KIBBUTZ.

Kibbutzniks were distressed by their decline in status. 'At one time,' Deborah said, 'you could walk into town just as you are, and people would point you out with envy and pride. There goes a kibbutznik. . . . But not today. Today we're looked at as characters. We don't dare go into town without dressing up and putting on make-up.'

Kofsky said, 'Once we were considered the élite, today we're looked on as hayseeds. In town they say we've abdicated our worries. You work eight hours a day, they say, you have food and security, and others worry for you.'

Life on a struggling kibbutz can be spartan. The chaverim work hard, very hard. Their farms generally have an alterior purpose too. They are usually dug into thinly populated areas, where it is in the strategic interest of Israel to have settlements.

Kofsky had little curiosity about the Canada he had left behind him.

'What's happening in Montreal? It's gotten bigger, that's all. All my friends are in Israel anyway. I guess we must seem very chauvinistic to you here. We're curious about everything in this country, it's ours, and we want to know all there is to know. The names of the different flowers and birds; and all the history.'

The day after the *seder* Gesher Haziv celebrated the Omer. Chaverim, guests and children crowded on to tractor wagons that had been decked out with flowers and started out on a bumpy ride that took us through all the fields of Gesher Haziv. As the group sang rousing songs we wheeled over wheat and cotton fields, the banana plantation, past workshops and the cemetery, finally pulling up at a field where the first wheat of the year was to be ceremoniously cut. The festivity had a forced folksy air to it, I'm afraid. The visiting Habonim Youth Group, Americans wearing Yemenite shirts, mounted a platform to perform harvest dances to the tune of a solitary flute. The rustic gesture clashed somewhat with the University of Syracuse sweatshirts and Bermuda shorts other youngsters were wearing, and the whirr of cameras as they avidly took moving pictures of one another.

Nobody at Gesher Haziv felt that the tourist motel, rapidly nearing completion, was a herald of decadence.

'We are a curiosity. Why shouldn't people come to see how we live?'

Two young boys shared the room next to mine. One of them, a twenty-two year old, had given up his American citizenship to become an Israeli.

'Why? Because I'm a Jew. I feel better here with my brothers the Yemenites. I have more in common with Iraqui and African Jews than I do with Irishmen in my home town.'

'Why didn't you settle on a Yemenite kibbutz, then?'

'I just sort of ended up here. Besides, the Yemenites hardly ever form kibbutzim. *They're* the sort who like the jingle of money in their pockets.'

Everywhere I went in Israel I asked about the Arabs.

Harvey Goodman, manager of the Eilat Hotel, said, 'It's got to be one thing or another. Either we develop a more enlightened Arab policy or we go to war and teach them a lesson. Next time we could take Cairo, set up a pro-Israeli government and move out again. They hate us, you know. They sit by the radios in their villages, listening to venomous broadcasts from Cairo. They stone our police cars and even tear down Israeli flags.' Goodman explained what he meant by a more enlightened policy. 'Educate them. We could integrate them and teach them that it's not such a bad thing to be an Arab in Israel.'

'Or a Jew in Canada?' I asked.

'No, sir. Never. You're always a Jew there. You know, there's actually no such thing as an "Arab". What, for instance, has an Arab in Cairo in common with a Bedouin from Iraq?'

'What have I got in common with a Yemenite Jew?'

'Jerusalem. All that the Arabs have in common is the fact that they're Moslem. Look here, the Americans could force them to sign a peace treaty with us any time they want to. They won't, though. We've been betrayed by the oil lobby in Washington.'

'Why don't the Arabs themselves want peace?'

'Because they need to maintain a war feeling within their own countries to keep the people's minds off their own miserable state.'

Bill Kofsky said, 'The trouble with the Arabs is they won't mix. They're private. They stick to their own people and areas. Another thing, you know, is they have loyalties outside the country.'

On the Mediterranean shore, at the foot of Gesher Haziv, lies the abandoned Arab village of Haziv. The fishermen of

Haziv fled during the war. Now an enterprising young Israeli lived in the village; he had made a museum and hopefully built a hostel and opened a nightclub. Haziv is mentioned in the Old Testament; Arab fishermen lived there even then. Wandering through its ruins two thousand years later one cannot help but feel guilty. This land belongs to the Arabs too.

The Arab settlements I visited in Israel were characterized by children with rickets, old men with trachoma, and ignorance and squalor everywhere. Take Ako, for instance. Once a Phoenician port, later a famous crusader stronghold, Ako is surrounded by a sea wall and towering fortifications. Barefoot kids scamper over the crumbling ramparts, leathery old men fish off the stone steps. Occasionally there was the surprise of a cool, delightful square with a fountain in the middle, but, for the most part, there were only the stinking narrow streets. Donkeys, chickens and other animals wandered somnolently through the maze of stalls in the marketplace. Barefoot boys flitted freely through the muck of decaying refuse and turds. The wares the vendors had to offer were pathetic. Rusty ancient locks, faded cotton dresses and split boots reclaimed from junk piles. Flies were everywhere.

Bill Kofsky had little patience with Ako. 'You think they're poor? Those guys own property everywhere. They have plenty of money.'

The souvenir shop I stopped at in Nazareth dealt in the usual bogus articles, water from Mary's Well and so forth. The enterprising Arab proprietor, however, also sold little bags of earth; half of them labelled 'Earth from the Holy Land, Nazareth', the printing superimposed over a cross; the others reading 'Earth from the Holy Land, Israel', a blue Star of David fixed above. I laughed. The Arab laughed. And it was with this shrewd irreverent Arab that the land of Israel came full circle for me. This Arab's gift for survival and self-evident humour seemed profoundly Jewish to me, more Jewish than the sabra. I could identify with him.

A lawyer I met in Jerusalem told me that he had served on the Gaza Strip when Israel had occupied the zone in 1956. 'Don't forget they've been there for fourteen years. Many have died out and others are not proper refugees at all. They were born in Gaza, they've never even seen Israel. The figure of one million is an inflated one too. When a man dies they don't hand in his ration book, but go on claiming his food.'

'But surely,' I said, 'if the Jews are entitled to come "home" after two thousand years then the son of an Arab refugee is a Palestinian too?'

'All right. Conditions in their camps are deplorable. However, the conditions I lived under in Dachau were worse.'